FIRST KNITS

Beautiful patterns for babies and young children

100 IDÉES

CONRAN OCTOPUS

Originally published as BABY KNITS in 1987 by
Conran Octopus Limited
37 Shelton Street
London WC2H 9HN

This revised edition published in 1991

The editors would like to thank Penny Hill
and Marilyn Wilson for their assistance.

British Library Cataloguing in Publication Data
First Knits: beautiful patterns for babies and young children.
    1. Children's clothing. Knitting
    I. 100 Idées
    646.407

ISBN 1 85029 345 7

Typeset by SX Composing Limited

Printed and bound in Hong Kong

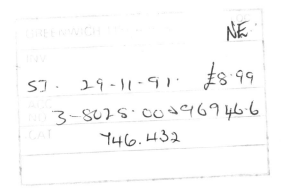

CONTENTS

BASIC ESSENTIALS 6

GEMINI GEM *two-tone reversible outfit* 8

CRADLED IN LUXURY *at the centre of the family* 12

ROSA MUNDI *pretty as a picture* 18

FAIR ISLE TRIO *warm, light and bright* 22

SLEEPY PIXIE LAYETTE *luxurious magic* 26

STRAWBERRY RIPE *and cherry sweet* 30

THE YOUNGEST CABIN BOY *smart sea-going outfit* 34

PASTEL PERFECTION *soft patchwork* 38

FIRST BEST OUTFIT *for an engaging and sociable baby* 44

STYLISH AND PRACTICAL *for a smart young man* 48

COLOURFUL CAROLINE *flowery twinset* 52

CALORIFIC COMFORT *for cold weather outings* 56

LITTLE PRINCE *sleep in comfort* 58

MIX AND MATCH SET *as easy as one, two, three* 62

STYLISH STRIPES *so easy a child could knit them* 66

APRIL TWOSOME *soft and fresh* 68

ANIMAL MAGIC *unlikely friends* 72

STOCKISTS AND ACKNOWLEDGMENTS 80

INTRODUCTION

Among the many reasons why babies are so popular is the undeniable truth that they provide avid knitters with a splendid excuse to indulge in their favourite pastime. In fact even people who have previously been non-knitters feel obliged to buy needles and yarn and at least attempt to make something when they learn that one of their family or circle of friends is expecting a baby. Here is a book full of entrancing and at the same time eminently practical patterns for babies and small children, with plenty to choose from, whether you are virtually a beginner or an experienced knitter.

The designs are all taken from the French magazine 100 IDEES, which is renowned for its innovative and highly attractive knitting patterns, and they all display that attention to detail combined with fashion flair that the French expect to see in their children's clothes. The necklines, for example, all make allowances for the comparatively large size of small children's heads, so there will be no yelps of discomfort as the sweaters are pulled on.

The clothes for slightly older infants are equally intelligently designed: the trousers on page 48 are knitted in a double thickness of yarn, to give firmness, while those on page 34 are knitted on smaller needles for the same effect, and the enchantingly pretty little girl's skirt on page 68 has an elasticated waist for an easy fit.

Some of the designs, such as the colourful striped top with matching blanket on page 66 or the mix-and-match outfits on page 62 should be well within the range of comparative beginners. Others, such as the rose-coloured sweater on page 18 – so charming that a good many adults would happily wear a scaled-up version – are for the more experienced knitter.

The soft, beautiful yarns used throughout will make these patterns a joy to knit, although it is perfectly possible to substitute other yarns, provided that you check the tension carefully, changing needles if necessary. Colours change with the seasons, and you may find that some of the colours used will eventually be replaced with other shades. But whatever combination you pick, you will find these clothes fun to make, just as the recipients will find them fun to wear, for they have been designed by people who love young children and who recognize them as small individuals.

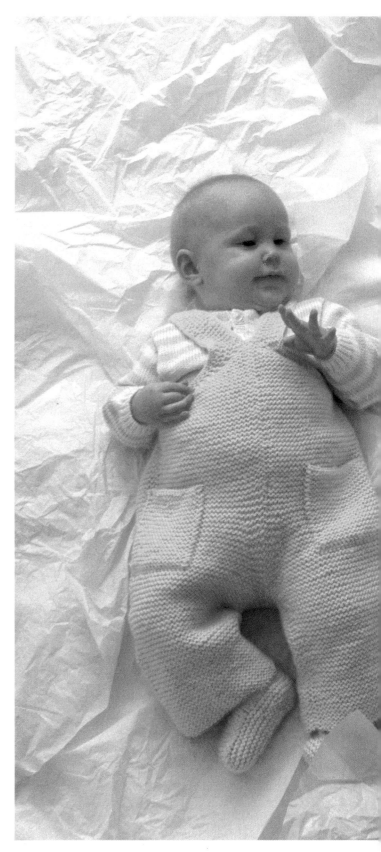

BASIC ESSENTIALS

One of the pleasures of knitting is that although the basic skills of casting on and off, knit and purl stitches are simple to learn, they lead to an almost infinite variety of patterns and textures, and the small scale of clothes for babies and young children makes them ideal practice pieces for anyone trying to expand her knitting repertoire. If any of the designs in this book include techniques with which you are unfamiliar, the following instructions are intended to show how they should be tackled. They also give details of the finishing touches which give a professional look.

YARNS
If you have difficulty in obtaining any of the yarns specified in the patterns, or where a yarn is available by mail order only, stockists' addresses are given on page 80. They will be able to give you the name of your local supplier or supply the yarn to you directly.

ABBREVIATIONS
The standard abbreviations used in this book are listed below. Any other abbreviations, used for a particular design, are given with the instructions.
k = knit
p = purl
st(s) = stitch(es)
st st = stocking stitch
rev st st = reverse stocking stitch
    (using p side as right side)
g st = garter stitch
rep = repeat
beg = beginning
patt = pattern
yfd = yarn forward
yrn = yarn round needle
tog = together
SKPO = slip 1, k 1, pass slipped
    st over
SKTPO = slip 1, k 2 tog, pass
    slipped st over
tbl = through back of loop (or
    loops)
kw = knitwise
pw = purlwise
cont = continue
rem = remaining
alt = alternate
foll = follow(s)(ing)
kfb (or pfb) = k (or p) into front
    and back of next st
inc = increase

dec = decrease
cm = centimetres
in = inches
d c = double crochet

TENSION
This is the most important part of any garment, yet it is the aspect which most knitters ignore. The designer has worked out the instructions on the basis of a particular tension and unless yours is exactly the same the finished garment will not be the correct size or shape, neither will the parts fit correctly together. The correct tension is given with each design and also the number of stitches which you should cast on to work a sample; by doing this you will be able to check that your tension is correct before starting the work and this will avoid disappointment later. Work the sample in the pattern given, or in stocking stitch if this is the basic pattern used; continue until the sample measures 12cm (5in) then cast off and measure the tension.

If your tension is not exactly right, try again using larger or smaller needles as necessary in order to obtain the correct tension. If you have more stitches

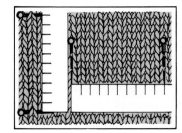

to 10cm (4in) than stated you are working too tightly and you should try larger needles; if you have fewer stitches you are working too loosely and you should try smaller needles. Use needles which produce the correct tension for the main parts of the garment, making corresponding alterations in the needle size(s) given for other parts such as ribbed borders or cuffs.

SIDES OF WORK
The first row worked after casting-on is always the right side unless otherwise stated. The expression 'front of work' refers to the side on which you are actually knitting and 'back' to the side away from you; these should not be confused with the terms 'right side' and 'wrong side' of work.

INCREASES AND DECREASES
To increase at the beginning of a row, either cast on a stitch or work into the front and back of the first stitch. To increase at the end of a row, work into the front and back of the last stitch. In this way it is easier to match the increases at the sides and thus make a neater seam. To decrease at the beginning of a row, either cast off a stitch or work SKPO. At the end of a row, work the last two stitches together.

DOUBLE YARN
For some designs yarn has to be used double. Using the two balls separately can result in an uneven appearance and it is easy to miss one of the strands. To avoid these difficulties, take a ball of the yarn and wind it into two balls of the same size, then rewind them together to form a double thickness ball.

SWISS DARNING
This is a popular and simple way of decorating garments by covering the stocking stitch, one stitch at a time, with a different colour or colours. The effect is the same as if the colours had been knitted in but it is much easier to

work. The method is used for embroidering the cherry and strawberry motifs in the designs on page 30 and for the contrasting patches on the cardigan (page 48). Some small sections of the pattern on the Fair Isle jacket (page 44) are also embroidered on by the same method. However it is not possible to use the Swiss darning method for other sections of this garment, nor can it be substituted for the Fair Isle pattern on the sweater trio shown on page 22, since allover Fair Isle gives a totally different tension.

Swiss darning can be worked either horizontally or vertically, whichever fits in most easily with the motif or pattern. If you are working isolated dots, simply carry the yarn across the back of the work as you would if knitting a Fair Isle pattern. Use a blunt-ended wool needle and, if you are using scrap-bag yarns, make sure that they are thick enough to cover the knitted stitches.

HORIZONTAL TECHNIQUE
Thread your needle and bring it out at the bottom right-hand corner of the motif, at the base of the first knitted stitch to be covered. Working from right to left, insert the needle behind the stitch immediately above.

Pull the yarn through, then insert the needle back through the base of the first stitch and bring it out at the base of the stitch immediately to the left.

Pull the yarn through, covering the first stitch, then work from right to left along the row.

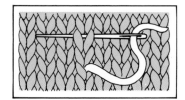

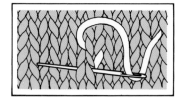

VERTICAL TECHNIQUE

This is worked more like chain-stitch embroidery, which Swiss darning closely resembles. Begin at the bottom, as for the horizontal technique, bringing the yarn through at the base of the first stitch and taking the needle from right to left behind the stitch above. Pull the yarn through and then insert the needle vertically behind the first stitch, as shown. Pull the yarn through to cover the first stitch and continue upwards.

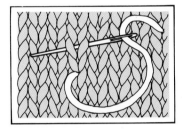

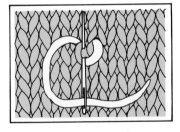

JACQUARD KNITTING

A few of the designs in this book are examples of the technique known as jacquard. The method of working is quite different from traditional Fair Isle in which two or more colours are carried across the row and used when needed. Jacquard designs either have motifs which may be small or large and are isolated against a background colour or else they have large panels or geometric shapes worked in various colours. In all these cases it is necessary to use separate balls of colour for each of the different motifs or shapes and, if these are large, a separate ball of the background colour is also needed for the stitches on each side. Join on the balls where necessary by making a single knot into the previous stitch; afterwards these knots can be unpicked and the ends darned in securely.

To avoid using whole balls of yarn wind off a small ball for each section; it is more convenient to wind them onto strips of cardboard. Cut a slit in the card so that the yarn can be passed through the slit when it is not being used. It will then hang without becoming entangled. All the spare colours are kept on the wrong side of the work and it is essential each time you begin with a new colour to pick it up from underneath the colour previously used so that it passes right around the previous colour. This will avoid holes forming in the work.

The technique requires practice to avoid the edges of the various sections becoming too loose.

FINISHING

Before sewing the garment together you may need to press the work, but check by consulting the ball-band. This will show by use of the conventional signs whether the yarn is one which can be pressed or not. Yarns that are composed of 100 per cent wool or 100 per cent cotton may be pressed by the method explained below but *do not* press garments knitted in garter stitch or in any pattern such as cable or those with a raised texture, or in any type of rib, as pressing would spoil the appearance. In these cases (also in the case of yarns where the actual knitting cannot be pressed) it is advisable to press the seams; again with reference to the ball-band, use either a warm iron and damp cloth or a cool iron and dry cloth and press very lightly using only the point of the iron.

If the yarn and the pattern permits whole sections to be pressed, blocking is a simple way of putting the pieces under a very slight tension during pressing. Fold a large towel or blanket to make a thick ironing pad, then lay the piece of knitting right side down on the pad. If there is a measurement diagram, check this as you pin the piece out, pulling it back into shape if it has become distorted. For a back or

front, start by pinning at the widest point, which is generally the chest measurement. Push the pins in right up to the head and position them about 1 cm (½in) apart all the way around the garment except at ribbed cuffs and hems, which are never pressed.

When the piece is pinned out, cover it with a clean cloth (damp or dry according to the instructions on the ball band): never put the iron directly on the knitting. Press very lightly, lifting the iron up and putting it down on new sections.

SEAMING

There are several methods of seaming and some are explained below. For most of the garments in this book the backstitch method is preferable, and it has the decided advantage of disguising any uneven edges and hiding the shapings such as shoulder casting off. Where a garment is made in garter stitch the flat seam method may be used instead; the various sections of the patchwork blanket (page 38) are also joined with a flat seam, these seams being afterwards covered by strips of knitting. Hems and facings should be slip-stitched in place.

For all seams use a blunt-ended wool needle or tapestry needle; this will avoid splitting the yarn – and your fingers.

METHOD 1 BACKSTITCH SEAM

Place the two pieces to be joined with right sides together and begin sewing at the right-hand end of the seam, securing the end of the yarn with two stitches, one on top of the other. Push the needle through both layers and bring it up to the top again. Push the needle in again at the starting

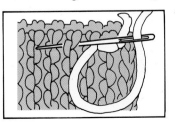

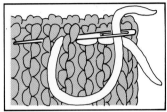

point and bring it out a little further from the point where you last brought it out to make one back-stitch. Continue backstitching to the end of the seam.

METHOD 2 FLAT SEAM

Start with right sides together and two stitches, as for the back-stitch seam. Carefully matching rows or stitches, and pushing the needle through vertically for greater accuracy, join the seam with a running stitch effect.

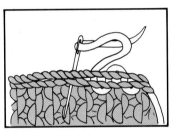

METHOD 3 INVISIBLE SEAMING

Place the two pieces right side up and side by side, matching the rows and edge stitches. Secure the end of the yarn at the bottom right-hand edge and pick up the matching stitch on the left-hand edge. Pull the yarn through tightly, then return to the right-hand edge and pick up the stitch on the next row up.

GEMINI GEM

Perfectly suited to the dual nature of a Gemini baby (22 May to 22 June), this two-tone outfit with accompanying blanket is completely reversible, a highly practical feature which will no doubt also appeal to those who are not addicted to star gazing and have their feet firmly planted on the ground. Quickly knitted in garter stitch on large needles, this is the ideal design for an inexperienced knitter.

CHECKLIST

JACKET, ROMPERS, HAT AND BOOTEES
Materials
*Brushed double knitting yarn: 6 × 50g balls each of 2 colours **A** and **B**. Pair each of needles size 4mm and 5mm; 4 buttons.*

Sizes
Three sizes, to fit ages 3 (6-9) months. Actual measurements shown on diagram.

Stitches used
Each garment is worked entirely in g st; k loop = pick up loop lying between needles and k it through the back.

Tension
Over g st using 5mm (larger) needles, 14 sts and 28 rows to 10cm (4in). Work a sample on 20 sts.

BLANKET
Materials
*Brushed double knitting yarn: 12 × 50g balls each of 2 colours **A** and **B**. Pair of needles size 4½mm.*

Size
Finished blanket measures 110cm (43½in) square.

Stitch used
Blanket is worked entirely in g st.

Tension
Over g st using 4½mm needles, 15 sts and 30 rows to 10cm (4in). Work a sample on 20 sts.

INSTRUCTIONS

JACKET

Section A (Work entirely in **A**.)
Main part Beg at front edge of left front cast on 24 (26-28) sts using larger needles and work in g st counting 1st row as right side. Work 48 (52-56) rows.✶✶
Using a short length of yarn cast on 26 (28-30) sts for sleeve. Return to main part.
▦ *Next row* K 24 (26-28) then onto same needle k the sts of

sleeve.
▦ *Next row* (wrong side) K 30 (32-34), turn leaving rem 20 (22-24) sts of main part unworked. Cont on the 30 (32-34) sts for sleeve and dec 1 st at both ends of every foll 6th row 3 (2-1) times then every foll 8th row 2 (3-4) times. Cont on rem 20 (22-24) sts until sleeve measures 15 (16-17)cm, 5⅞ (6¼-6¾)in, from beg. Cast off loosely.
▦ **Back** Fold sleeve in half and pick up and k 4 sts along the

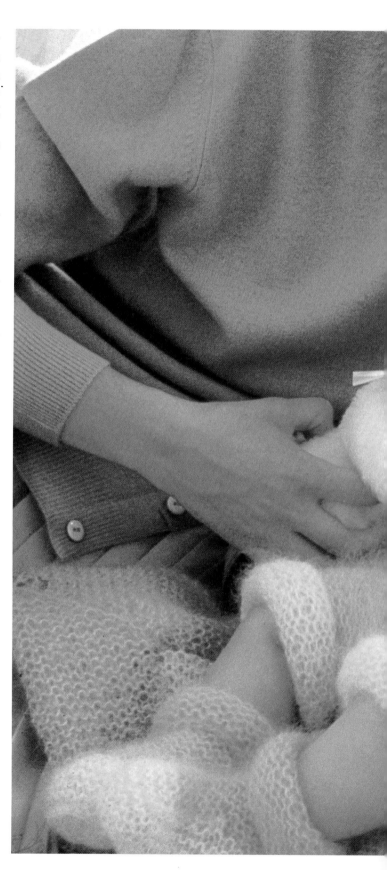

outer 4 sts of those cast on for sleeve then onto same needle with wrong side facing k the 20 (22-24) sts of main part which were left unworked.✲✲ Cont on 24 (26-28) sts and work 68 (74-80) rows. Now work exactly as for left sleeve from ✲✲ to ✲✲. You now have 24 (26-28) sts for right front. Cont on these sts and work 48 (52-56) rows. Cast off loosely.

▥ **Yoke** With right side facing and using larger needles, pick up and k 26 (28-30) sts along upper edge of right front, 22 (24-26) sts along upper edge of right sleeve, 36 (38-40) sts along upper edge of back, 22 (24-26) sts along upper edge of left sleeve and 26 (28-30) sts along upper edge of left front. 132 (142-152) sts. Cont in g st across all sts; k 1 row then begin shaping.

▥ *1st row* K 26 (28-30), SKTPO, k 16 (18-20), k 3 tog, k 36 (38-40), SKTPO, k 16 (18-20), k 3 tog, k 26 (28-30).

▥ *2nd and alt rows* K.

▥ *3rd row* K 26 (28-30), SKTPO, k 12 (14-16), k 3 tog, k 36 (38-40), SKTPO, k 12 (14-16), k 3 tog, k 26 (28-30). Work double decs in same positions on next 2 alt rows working 4 sts fewer between pairs of decs each time. Work 1 row on rem 100 (110-120) sts. Change to smaller needles and work neck border.

▥ *1st row* K 4 (5-6), [k 2 tog, k 5] 13 (14-15) times, k 2 tog, k 3 (5-7).

▥ *2nd and alt rows* K.

▥ *3rd row* K 3 (4-6), [k 2 tog, k 4] 13 (14-15) times, k 2 tog, k 3 (5-6).

▥ *5th row* K 3 (4-6), [k 2 tog, k 3] 13 (14-15) times, k 2 tog, k 2 (4-5).

▥ *7th row* K 2 (4-5), [k 2 tog, k 2] 13 (14-15) times, k 2 tog, k 2 (3-5). Cont on rem 44 (50-56) sts and work 4 rows without shaping then cast off firmly.

Section B (Working entirely in **B**) work each part as for Section A.)

▥ **Finishing** Join sleeve seams of each section. Place one section inside the other so that right sides of each are tog. Sew sections tog along outer edge of sleeves, all around neck and front edges and along lower edge leaving a space at centre back. Turn right side out and neatly close opening.

ROMPERS

Section A (Worked entirely in **A**.)

▥ **Front** For one leg cast on 14 (15-16) sts using larger needles and work in g st counting 1st row as right side. Work 6(7-8)cm, 2⅜(2¾-3⅛)in, ending with a wrong-side row. Inc 1 st at beg of next row then cont on these 15 (16-17) sts until work measures 11(12-13)cm, 4¼(4¾-5⅛)in, from beg, ending at shaped edge. Cut yarn and leave sts on a spare needle. Work second leg in same way but working the inc at opposite edge; cont until you have worked same number of rows ending at straight edge.

▥ *Next row* K 15(16-17), turn, cast on 4(5-5) sts, turn, then beg at shaped edge k 15(16-17) sts of first leg. Cont on these 34(37-39) sts until work measures 26(28-30)cm, 10¼(11-11¾)in, from beg then change to smaller needles and cont until front measures 29(31-33)cm, 11⅜(12¼-13)in, from beg, ending with a wrong-side row. ✲✲

▥ **Neck Shaping** *Next row* Cast off 4, k until there are 11 (12-13) sts on right needle, leave these sts of left front on a holder, cast off next 4 (5-5) sts, k until there are 11 (12-13) sts on right needle for right front, cast off rem 4 sts and fasten off. Rejoin yarn to sts of right front and dec 1 st at both ends of every alt row until 3 (2-3) sts rem. Cast off. Complete left front in same way.

▥ **Back** Work as for front to ✲✲.

▥ *Next row* Cast off 7 (8-9), k until there are 4 sts on right needle, place these sts onto a safety pin for right shoulder strap, cast off next 12 (13-13) sts, k until there are 4 sts on right needle, cast off rem 7 (8-9) sts and fasten off. Rejoin yarn to second group of 4 sts and using smaller needles cont in g st for left shoulder strap. Work 14(15-16)cm, 5½(5⅞-6¼)in, then make buttonhole.

▦ *Next row* K 2 tog, yfd, k 2. Work 2 more rows then cast off. Work right shoulder strap in same way.

Section B (Working entirely in **B**, work front and back as for section A.)

▦ **Finishing** Join inner leg and crotch seams of Section A then join side seams. Repeat for Section B. Place one section inside the other with right sides tog. Join sections all around upper edges. Turn right side out and neatly sew the sections tog around lower edge of legs. Oversew the straps of each section tog and buttonhole st around double buttonholes. Sew a button to top of each front, on A section and 2 more on B section so that straps can be fastened through buttons on both sides.

BOOTEES

▦ These are single thickness. Using smaller needles and **A** cast on 29 (31-33) sts for centre of sole and work in g st; work 2 rows without shaping.

▦ *3rd row* K 1, k loop, k 13 (14-15), k loop, k 1, k loop, k 13 (14-15), k loop, k 1.

▦ *4th row* K.

▦ *5th row* K 1, k loop, k 14 (15-16), k loop, k 3, k loop, k 14 (15-16), k loop, k 1. Cont on these 37 (39-41) sts and work 13 (15-17) rows.

▦ **Instep Shaping** *1st row* K 21 (22-23), k 2 tog, turn, thus leaving 14 (15-16) sts unworked.

▦ *2nd row* Slip 1, k 5, k 2 tog, turn leaving 14 (15-16) sts at this edge also. Rep 2nd row twice more, thus taking in 1 st from those at side each time. Change to **B** and rep 2nd row 12 times more. Turn after last row and k to end. Cont on 21 (23-25) sts and work 26 (28-30) rows then cast off loosely.

▦ Fold cast-on edge in half and join with a flat seam. Sew back seam of bootee reversing it for turnover top. If you choose, you

can outline the sole with a row of crochet as folls: using a medium-sized crochet hook and **A**, work a row of d c along the ridge formed by 8th (10th-12th) row of g st from beg.

HAT

Section A (Work entirely in **A**.)

▦ Using larger needles cast on 56 (60-64) sts and work in g st; cont until hat measures 14(15-16)cm, 5½ (5⅞-6¼)in, from beg, then shape top.

▦ *1st row* K 3, [k 2 tog, k 2] 13 (14-15) times, k 1. Work 3 rows without shaping.

▦ *5th row* K 2, [k 2 tog, k 1] 13 (14-15) times, k 2. K 1 row.

▦ *7th row* [K 2 tog] 15 (16-17) times. K 1 row.

▦ *9th row* [K 2 tog] 7 (8-8) times, k 1 (0-1). Cut yarn; thread end through rem sts; draw up tightly and sew securely, then join back seam.

Section B (Working entirely in **B**, work as for Section A.)

▦ **Finishing** Place one hat inside the other with right sides tog and seams level; oversew around cast-on edges leaving a space at back, turn right side out and neatly close opening. Sew the two layers tog with a few sts at top of hat.

BLANKET

▦ **Main Part** Using **A** cast on 136 sts and work in g st for 90cm (35½in).

▦ Cast off.

▦ Work another section in the same way using **B**.

▦ **Border** Using **A** cast on 16 sts and work in g st for 90cm (35½in) then shape corner.

▦ ✳✳ *1st row* Count this as right side of work. K 15, turn.

▦ *2nd and alt rows* Slip 1, k to end.

▦ *3rd row* K 14, turn.

▦ *5th row* K 13, turn. Cont working 1 st fewer on every alt row until 27th row has been worked on 2 sts; rep 2nd row.

▦ *29th row* K 3, turn.

▦ *30th row* As 2nd. Work 1 more st before turning on every alt row until you are working across the full 16 sts. Cont in g st across all sts for 90cm (35½in) ending at outer edge after a wrong-side row. ✳✳ Rep from ✳✳ to ✳✳ twice more.

▦ Shape last corner as before and when 1 row has been worked on 16 sts cast off.

▦ Make another border using **B**.

▦ **Finishing** Backstitch cast-on and cast-off edges of each border strip. With right sides tog backstitch border worked in **B** around main part worked in **A** and border in **A** around main part in **B**.

▦ Hold the two sections with wrong sides inside and join by oversewing all around outer edges, taking small neat sts between the rows of g st on border.

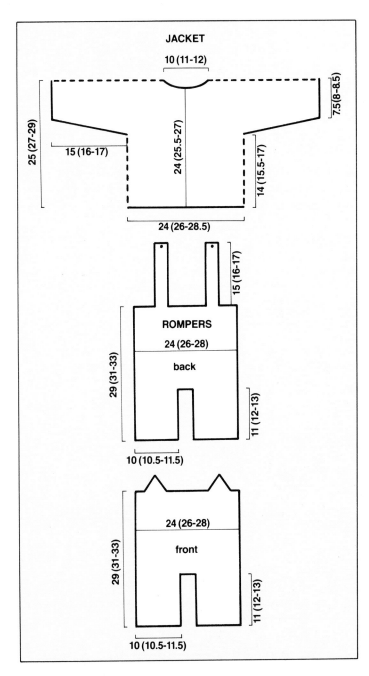

JACKET

10 (11-12)

7.5 (8-8.5)

25 (27-29)

15 (16-17)

24 (25.5-27)

14 (15.5-17)

24 (26-28.5)

15 (16-17)

ROMPERS

24 (26-28)

back

29 (31-33)

11 (12-13)

10 (10.5-11.5)

24 (26-28)

front

29 (31-33)

11 (12-13)

10 (10.5-11.5)

CRADLED IN LUXURY

This easy yet interesting pattern of knit and purl checks makes an ideal set for the baby who has everything, including three brothers and sisters to spoil him. Made in a soft 4-ply yarn, the set consists of a warm wraparound jacket with an overlap at the back, trousers with an adjustable waist to fit most new-born babies, and matching socks to add a cosy finishing touch. New babies generally sleep on their fronts (to lessen the risk of choking), so the back opening will be a particularly comfortable and welcome feature.

CHECKLIST

Materials
Sirdar Country Style 4-ply: 4(5-5) × 50g balls cream for the set. Pair each of needles size 2¾mm and 3¼mm; a set of double-pointed needles size 3¼mm for socks; a cable needle; 2 buttons for jacket.

Sizes
Three sizes, to fit ages 3 (6-9) months. Actual measurements shown on diagram. Socks, in one size only, fit a baby up to 6 months.

Stitches used
Single rib; st st; p g st = *purl garter stitch, p every row;* patt, *worked on a multiple of 10 sts plus 5 as foll:*
  1st row *(right side)* * K 5, p 5; * *rep from* * *to* * *ending k 5.*
  2nd row *P.*
  3rd to 8th rows *Rep 1st and 2nd rows 3 times more.*
  9th row * *P 5, k 5;* * *rep from* * *to* * *ending p 5.*
  10th row *P.*
  11th to 16th rows *Rep 9th and 10th rows 3 times more. These 16 rows form one patt. This patt is arranged differently on each section according to size as explained in the instructions. Work a sample first in order to become familiar with the patt.*
Cable panel, *worked on right front of wraparound jacket, on 10 sts as foll:*
  1st row *P 2, k 6, p 2.*
  2nd and alt rows *K 2, p 6, k 2.*
  3rd row *P 2, slip next 3 sts on cable needle, leave at back, k 3, then k 3 from cable needle, p 2.*
  5th row *As 1st.*
  7th row *P 2, k 1, yfd, k 2 tog, k 3, p 2.*
  9th row *P 2, SKPO, yfd, k 4, p 2.*
  11th row *As 7th.*
  13th row *As 1st.*
  15th row *As 3rd.*
  17th row *As 1st.*
  19th row *P 2, k 3, SKPO, yfd, k 1, p 2.*
  21st row *P 2, k 4, yfd, k 2 tog, p 2.*
  23rd row *As 19th.*
  24th row *As 2nd. These 24 rows form one patt; see instructions for placing of this panel.*

Tension
Over patt using 3¼mm needles, 26 sts and 44 rows to 10cm (4in). Work a sample on 35 sts as given above.

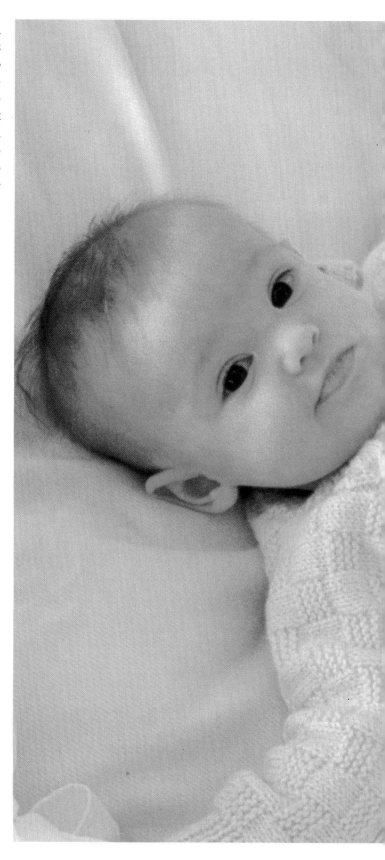

INSTRUCTIONS

WRAPAROUND JACKET

Main Part This is worked in one piece, with an opening at the back. With smaller needles cast on 59 (65-69) sts for front welt and work in rib.

▦ *1st row* (right side) P 1, * k 1, p 1; rep from * to end.

▦ *2nd row* K 1, * p 1, k 1; rep from * to end. Rep these 2 rows 4 times more, then 1st row again. Change to larger needles and p 1 row on wrong side working 1 inc at centre. 60 (66-70) sts. Now work in check patt with cable panel as foll:

▦ *1st row* P 0 (3-5), [k 5, p 5] 3 times, k 5, work 1st row of cable panel over next 10 sts, k 5, p 5, k 5, p 0 (3-5).

▦ *2nd row* P 15 (18-20), work 2nd row of cable panel, p 35 (38-40). Work 6 more rows as now set taking care to keep cable panel correct.

▦ *9th row* K 0 (3-5), [p 5, k 5] 3 times, p 5, work cable panel, p 5, k 5, p 5, k 0 (3-5).

▦ *10th row* P 15 (18-20), work cable panel, p 35 (38-40). Work 6 more rows with check patt as now set. These 16 rows form check patt for sts on each side of cable panel. Cont in patt for a further 28 (32-36) rows.

▦ **Sleeve Shaping** Cast on 5 (7-10) sts at beg of next 2 rows, 10 sts at beg of next 4 rows and 11 sts at beg of next 2 rows working extra sts into patt. When all extra sts have been added there will be a complete check at each side plus 1 border st which should be worked p on every row. Cont on 132 (142-152) sts and work 12 (16-20) rows in patt; 64 (72-80) rows have now been worked in patt.

▦ **Neck Shaping** *Next row* Patt 62 (66-70) sts and leave these sts of left front on a spare needle, cast off next 8 (10-12) sts, patt to end. Cont on 62 (66-70) sts now rem on needle for right front and work 1 row. ** Cast off 3 sts at beg of next row, 2 sts at same edge on next 2 alt rows and 1 st on next 3 alt rows. ** The cable panel has now been eliminated; cont in check patt and work 3 rows without shaping; a total of 80 (88-96) rows has now been worked in patt. Place marker loop of contrast yarn at side edge to indicate shoulder line then cont for right back.

▦ Work 2 rows without shaping thus ending at neck edge then shape back neck; *** cast on 1 st at beg of next row and next alt row, 2 sts at same edge on next 2 alt rows, 4 sts on next alt row and 8 (9-10) sts on next alt row. Take

the first 14 (15-16) sts added into patt thus forming complete checks, then the rem 4 sts should be worked in p g st to form a border for back. Cont on these 70 (75-80) sts and work 16 (20-24) rows without shaping thus ending at sleeve edge then cast off 11 sts at beg of next row, 10 sts at same edge on next 2 alt rows and 5 (7-10) sts on next alt row. ***

▦ Cont on rem 34 (37-39) sts with patt at side edge matching side of front and work 44 (48-52) rows; 80 (88-96) rows have been worked on right back, ending with an 8th or 16th patt row. **** K 1 row working 1 dec at centre for 1st size only. Change to smaller needles and cont on 33 (37-39) sts; beg with 2nd row work in rib as on front welt for 11 rows then cast off loosely ribwise.

▦ **Left Front** With wrong side facing and using larger needles rejoin yarn at neck edge to sts of left front and cont in check patt shaping as for right front from ** to ** then work 4 rows without shaping thus reaching shoulder line. Place marker at side edge then cont for left back and work 1 row straight thus ending at neck edge. Now work as for right back from *** to *** then cont on rem 34 (37-39) sts and work 45 (49-

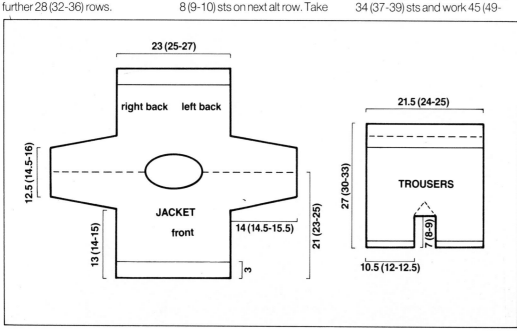

23 (25-27)

right back   left back

12.5 (14.5-16)

JACKET

front

13 (14-15)

14 (14.5-15.5)

21 (23-25)

3

21.5 (24-25)

27 (30-33)

TROUSERS

7 (8-9)

10.5 (12-12.5)

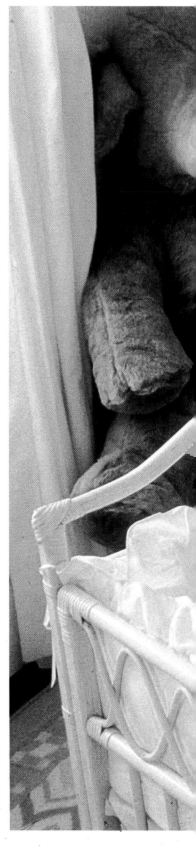

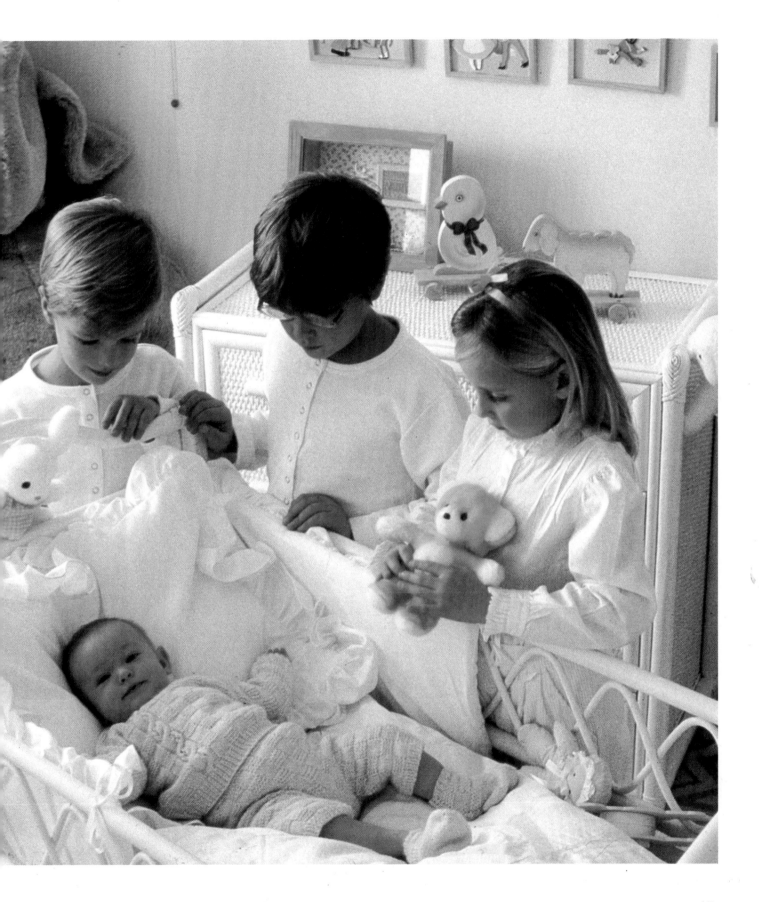

53) rows thus ending with same row of patt as on right back. Complete as for right back from **** to end.

■ **Cuffs** With right side of work facing and using smaller needles, pick up and k 31 (35-37) sts along outer edge of one sleeve. Beg with 2nd row work 11 rows in rib then cast off loosely in rib. Work similar cuff on other sleeve.

■ **Neck Border** With right side facing and using smaller needles, pick up and k 26 (27-28) sts across left back neck edge, 45 (47-49) sts around front neck and 26 (27-28) sts across right back neck. 97 (101-105) sts. K 1 row on wrong side then beg with 1st row work 5 rows in rib. Cast off loosely in rib.

■ **Finishing** Join side and sleeve seams matching patt. Make a buttonhole loop at each back neck edge and sew on buttons to correspond, one on wrong side of work and one on

right side so that one side of back laps over the other.

TROUSERS

■ **Back** With smaller needles cast on 27 (31-33) sts for first leg and work 5 rows in rib as on back then change to larger needles and p 1 row on wrong side working 1 inc at centre for 1st size. Cont on these 28 (31-33) sts in patt as foll:
■ *1st row* This begins at inner leg edge. K 5 (0-0), [p 5, k 5] 2 (3-3) times, p 3 (1-3). Cont in patt as now set for a further 23 (27-31) rows thus ending at inner leg edge. Cut yarn and leave sts on a spare needle. Work second leg in same way for 6 rows then work in patt.
■ *1st row* This begins at outer edge. K 3 (1-3), [p 5, k 5] 2 (3-3) times, p 5 (0-0). Cont in patt as now set for a further 23 (27-31) rows thus ending at outer edge. Now join legs.
■ *Next row* Patt 28 (31-33) sts of second leg, turn, cast on 18 (20-

22) sts for gusset, then with right side facing patt the sts of first leg. 74 (82-88) sts. Keep sts of gusset in st st and sts on each side in patt; p 1 row then begin shaping gusset.
■ *Next row* Patt 28 (31-33), SKPO, k 14 (16-18), k 2 tog, patt 28 (31-33). Cont to dec at beg and end of gusset sts working 2 sts fewer between decs each time, on next 7 (8-9) alt rows; p 1 row on rem 58 (64-68) sts.
■ *Next row* Patt 27 (30-32), k 3 tog, patt 28 (31-33). Cont on rem 56 (62-66) sts working all sts in check patt until work measures 21 (24-27)cm, 8¼(9½-10⅝)in, from beg, ending with a p row, and dec 1 st in centre of this last row. 55 (61-65) sts. Change to smaller needles and work in rib; after working 8 rows make holes for cord.
■ *Next row* [P 1, k 1, yfd, k 2 tog] 13 (15-16) times, rib 3 (1-1). Cont in rib until this border measures 6cm (2⅜in). Cast off in rib.

■ **Front** Work as for back.

■ **Finishing** Backstitch side seams and inner leg seams matching patt; join cast-on edges of gusset with a flat seam. Make a length of crochet or twisted cord and insert through holes at waist to tie in front.

SOCKS

■ Beg at leg edge cast on 31 sts using smaller needles. Work 5 rows in rib then change to larger needles and p 1 row working 1 inc at centre. 32 sts. Now work in patt with 1 border st each side.
■ *1st row* P 1, [k 5, p 5] 3 times, p 1. Cont in patt as now set for 23 more rows. Now work in st st; work 2 rows then divide for heel. Cut yarn, slip 8 sts onto a holder, slip next 16 sts onto a piece of contrast yarn, now k next 8 sts and onto same needle k the first group of 8 sts. Cont on these 16 sts for heel, work 9 more rows in st st then shape heel.
■ *1st row* K 11, SKPO, turn leaving 3 sts unworked.
■ *2nd row* P 7, p 2 tog, turn leaving 3 sts unworked.
■ *3rd row* K 7, SKPO, turn.
■ *4th row* P 7, p 2 tog, turn. Rep last 2 rows twice more; all sts at sides have been worked in and 8 sts rem. Now take the set of double-pointed needles and beg working in rounds of st st = k every round.
■ *1st round* K the 8 sts of heel, pick up and k 8 sts along side edge of heel, k the 16 sts of instep, pick up and k 8 sts along other side of heel, now k first 4 sts of heel so that rounds will begin and end at centre of heel.
■ *2nd round* K without shaping.
■ *3rd round* K 10, k 2 tog, k 16, SKPO, k 10. Cont to dec at each side of the instep sts on next 2 alt rounds then cont on rem 34 sts and work 3cm (1⅛in) then shape toe.
■ *1st round* K 7, k 2 tog, k 16, SKPO, k 7. Cont to dec in same positions as before on next 2 alt rounds then on foll 3 rounds.
■ *Next round* [K 2 tog] 11 times. Cut yarn, pass end through rem sts, draw up tightly and sew securely; darn in end. Make a neat seam along back of leg.

ROSA MUNDI

Say it with roses: knit a minor labour of love for the one you love. Three shades of pink in a beautifully soft yarn are used for this chic and very feminine little sweater with its intriguingly irregular combination of checks, stripes and panels and a single cable to one side of the neck. The blue spots are embroidered on afterwards, so the pattern is not quite as difficult as it might look. An opening on the left shoulder allows for easy dressing and buttons up for a snug fit. It is heartbreaking when a baby grows out of a pretty garment too soon, so if you are knitting for a child that is still to arrive, and you suspect that it may be large at birth, play safe and choose a larger size.

CHECKLIST

Materials
*Brushed double knitting yarn, one × 50g ball in each of the foll colours: pale pink (**A**), mid pink (**B**), and deep pink (**C**). A small amount of blue embroidery cotton is used for the spots.*
Pair each of needles size 3¼mm and 4mm; a cable needle; 3 small buttons.

Sizes
Three sizes, to fit ages 3 (6-9 to 12) months. Actual measurements shown on diagram.

Stitches used
Double rib; st st; patt, worked from charts. Use separate small balls or short lengths of the shades for each different section, joining them on as required and taking care to twist yarns around each other on wrong side when changing colour during a row.
*Cable Panel, worked on 6 sts in **B** as shown on charts.*
  1st row P 1, k 4, p 1.
  2nd row K 1, p 4, k 1.
  3rd and 4th rows As 1st and 2nd.
  5th row P 1, slip next 2 sts on cable needle, leave at back, k 2, then k 2 from cable needle, p 1.
  *6th to 10th rows Rep 2nd row once then 1st and 2nd rows twice more. These 10 rows form one patt for this panel. After working this panel ensure that **B** yarn is taken through to wrong side of work.*
Note *This sweater is worked in one piece beginning at the lower edge of the front and ending at the lower edge of the back; cuffs are worked on afterwards.*

Tension
Over st st using 4mm needles, 20 sts and 30 rows to 10cm (4in). Work a sample on 26 sts.

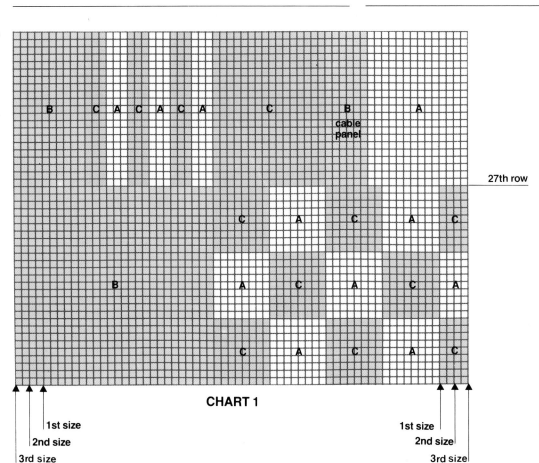

27th row

CHART 1

1st size
2nd size
3rd size

1st size
2nd size
3rd size

INSTRUCTIONS

Main Part With smaller needles and **A**, cast on 54 (58-62) sts and work in rib.
  1st row (right side) K 2, * p 2, k 2; rep from * to end.
  2nd row P 2, * k 2, p 2; rep from * to end. Cont in this rib working 4 rows **B** then 4 rows **C** and inc 1 st at both ends of last rib row. 56 (60-64) sts. Change to larger needles and working in st st work patt from Chart No 1, joining small balls of colours as needed.
  1st row K 0 (2-4) **C**, [8 **A**, 8 **C**] twice, 24 (26-28) **B**. Cont working from chart as now set always twisting yarns around

Key
A = *pale pink*
B = *mid pink*
C = *deep pink*

Begin and end at position indicated according to size. Begin on 1st row of chart and continue until 36 (42-48) rows have been worked then begin sleeve shapings as explained in the instructions.

18

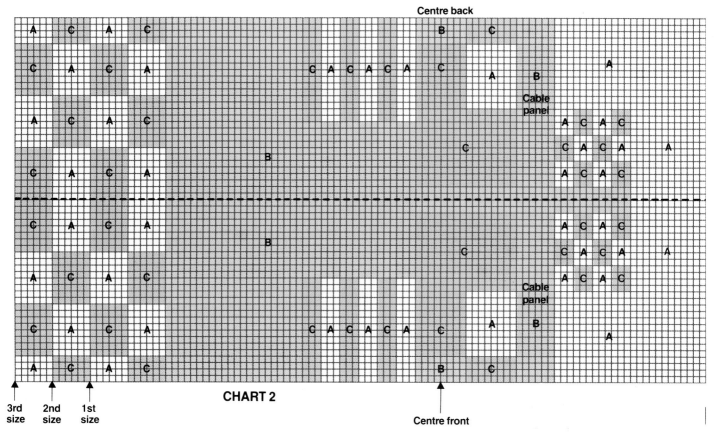

Centre back

Cable panel

Cable panel

CHART 2

3rd size 2nd size 1st size

Centre front

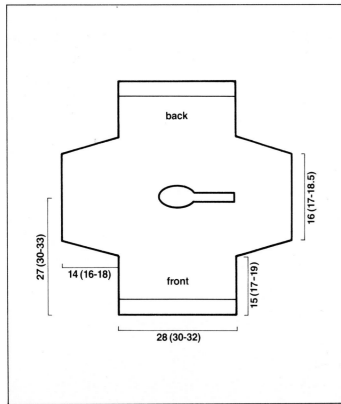

back

16 (17-18.5)

27 (30-33)

14 (16-18)

front

15 (17-19)

28 (30-32)

each other when changing colour. When 27th row has been worked begin next section.

▦ *28th row* P 6 (8-10) **B**, [3 **C**, 3 **A**] 3 times, 16 **C**, 6 **B**, 10 (12-14) **A**. Beg on foll row work cable panel as explained above on the group of 6 sts in **B** and cont in patt as now set until 36 (42-48) rows have been worked from beg of this chart.

▦ **Sleeve Shaping** Cont with colours as set and cast on 4 sts at beg of next 2 (6-8) rows (then 5 sts at beg of next 2 rows for 3rd size only); keep the extra sts added at sides in same colour as side panels. 64 (84-106) sts. Now begin a square in **B** at centre.

▦ *Next row* Using **A**, cast on 4 (5-5) sts, k these sts and next 14 (24-35) sts in **A**, now work the cable panel in **B**, then k 8 **C**, 8 **B**, [3 **A**, 3 **C**] 3 times, 10 (20-31) **B**. Keeping all colours as set cast on 4 (5-5) sts at beg of next row then 5 sts at beg of next 8 (6-4) rows keeping the extra sts added at sides in same colour as side panels. 112 (124-136) sts. Now

work from Chart No 2 beg with 5th (3rd-1st) row of chart; work 12 (14-16) rows.

▦ **Neck Shaping** *17th row of chart* Patt 52 (57-62) and leave these sts of left front on a spare needle, cast off next 8 (10-12) sts, patt to end. Cont on 52 (57-62) sts now rem on needle for right front. Dec 1 st at neck edge on next 2 rows then at same edge on next 3 alt rows. Work 3 rows on rem 47 (52-57) sts; 28th row of chart has now been worked and shoulder level is reached.

▦ Cont on same sts for right back; work 2 rows without shaping thus ending at neck edge then cast on 6 sts at beg of next row. Work 1 row thus ending at neck edge then leave these 53 (58-63) sts on a spare needle.

▦ With wrong side facing return to sts of left front and cont in patt; dec 1 st at neck edge on next 2 rows then at same edge on next 3 alt rows.

▦ *26th row of chart* Cast off 20 sts to form shoulder opening, patt to end. Work 2 rows on rem

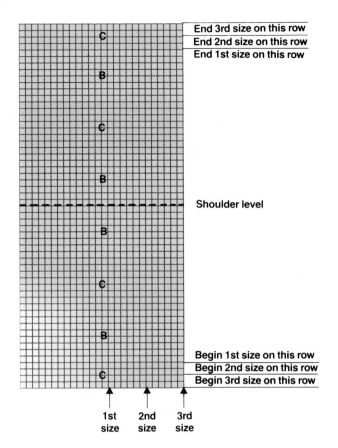

End 3rd size on this row
End 2nd size on this row
End 1st size on this row

C

B

C

B

Shoulder level

B

C

B

Begin 1st size on this row
Begin 2nd size on this row
Begin 3rd size on this row

C

| 1st size | 2nd size | 3rd size |

Chart shows full width of sweater including sleeves. Begin and end at the position indicated and on the row indicated according to size being worked. The dotted line across the centre of the chart indicates shoulder level; the neck opening is not shown as this is different for each size and is explained in the instructions.

■ **Cuffs** With right side of work facing and using smaller needles and **A**, pick up and k 30 (34-38) sts along outer edge of one sleeve. Beg with 2nd row work in rib as on welt working 4 rows **C**, 4 rows **B** and 2 rows **A**. Cast off in rib. Work other cuff in same way.

■ **Neck and Shoulder Borders** With right side of work facing using smaller needles and **B**, pick up and k 26 (28-30) sts around front neck edge and 20 (22-24) sts across back neck. 46 (50-54) sts. Beg with 2nd row work in rib for 6 rows using **B** only; cast off in rib. With right side of work facing using smaller

needles and **B**, pick up and k 26 sts along left front shoulder edge including edge of neck border. Beg with 2nd row work in rib and after working 2 rows make buttonholes.

■ *Next row* Beg at neck edge, wrong side facing, rib 2, cast off 2, [rib until there are 6 sts on right needle after previous buttonhole, cast off 2] twice, rib to end. On foll row cast on 2 sts over each buttonhole. Work 2 more rows then cast off in rib. Work similar border on left back but omitting buttonholes.

■ **Finishing** Join side and sleeve seams matching patt. Overlap front shoulder border on back border and sew ends to side of shoulder opening. Sew buttons to back border to correspond with buttonholes.

■ Using blue embroidery cotton form spots on the large **B** section at beg of right front and the small **B** square at centre of neckline working a group of French knots close tog. Work spots in same positions on back.

27 (32-37) sts thus reaching shoulder level then cont for left back and work next 2 rows of chart. Using a short length of **B** cast on 20 sts onto a spare needle; return to sts of left back.
■ *31st row* Patt 27 (32-37), then working across 20 sts just cast on, k 0 (0-1) **A**, 2 (3-3) **C**, 3 **A**, 3 **C**, 3 **A**, then with **B** work 1st row of cable panel on next 6 sts, then k 3 (2-1) **C**. Keeping patt correct cast on 6 sts at beg of next row.
■ *33rd row* Patt 53 (58-63), turn, cast on 6 (8-10) sts, turn, then patt across sts of right back. 112 (124-136) sts. Cont in patt across all sts and work 19 (21-23) rows thus ending with the 52nd (54th-56th) row of chart.
■ **Sleeve Shaping** *1st row* Using **A** cast off 5, k until there are 33 (39-45) sts on right needle, work cable panel in **B**, then k 8 **C**, 8 **B**, [3 **A**, 3 **C**] 3 times, then k rem 34 (40-46) sts. Keeping side sections in **A** and **B** and the stripes and panels as on this row, cast off 5 sts at beg of next 7 (7-5) rows then for 1st size only cast off

4 sts at beg of next 2 rows. 64 (84-106) sts.
■ *Next row* Using **A** cast off 4 (4-5), k until there are 10 (20-30) sts on right needle, work cable panel in **B** then k 16 **C**, [3 **A**, 3 **C**] 3 times, k 10 (20-31) **B**. Cont in patt as set and complete sleeve shaping by casting off for 1st size 4 sts at beg of foll row (for 2nd size 4 sts at beg of next 5 rows; for 3rd size 5 sts at beg of next row and 4 sts at beg of next 8 rows). 56 (60-64) sts. Cont with patt as given at top of Chart No 1 and work 9 (15-21) rows without shaping thus ending with a right-side row. Discontinue the cable panel and work all sts in st st, working first 27 rows of chart; as next row is a p row begin at left-hand edge of chart and patt ends on a p row. Change to smaller needles and **C**; k 1 row and dec 1 st at each end; cont on rem 54 (58-62) sts in rib as on front welt beg with 2nd row working 3 rows in **C** then 4 rows **B** and 2 rows **A**. Cast off in rib using **A**.

FAIR ISLE TRIO

An eye-catching trio of sweaters makes a wonderful gift for three young triplets, cousins or friends. All have the same basic shape, but each one has a different colour pattern. The sweater with the blue collar, which uses only four colours, instead of the eight used in each of the others, would make a relatively simple introduction to Fair Isle knitting for a beginner moving on to this more complicated technique. The fine mohair yarn is used double stranded throughout, for extra warmth without weight.

CHECKLIST

Materials

STYLE 1
For Style 1, with yellow collar, in centre of picture, Pingouin Sweet'hair, one × 50g ball in each of the foll colours: bright pink (A), deep pink (B), bright blue (C), sea green (D), deep green (E), bright red (F), yellow (G), deep blue (H).
Pair each of needles size 4mm and 5mm.
2 small buttons.

STYLE 2
For Style 2, with pink collar, left of picture: yarns, needles and buttons as above.

STYLE 3
For Style 3, with blue collar, right of picture: one × 50g ball in each of colours B, C, D and G, plus needles and buttons as for Style 1.

Sizes
Three sizes, to fit ages 3 (6-9) months. Actual measurements shown on diagram.

Stitches used
Single rib; st st; patt, *worked from charts as explained below.*
Note *Yarn is used double throughout: take each ball and wind it into two equal balls then rewind these into a double stranded ball which will be easier to use.*

Tension
Over patt using 5mm needles and yarn double, 18 sts and 20 rows to 10cm (4in). Work a sample on 23 sts as for 2nd size on Style 3.

INSTRUCTIONS

STYLE 1

Back With smaller needles and **E** (wound into a double-stranded ball as described above), cast on 39 (43-47) sts and work in rib.
▦ ** *1st row* (right side) P 1, * k 1, p 1; rep from * to end.
▦ *2nd row* K 1, * p 1, k 1; rep from * to end. Rep these 2 rows 1 (2-3) times more then 1st row again; 5 (7-9) rows worked. **
▦ *Inc row* P 4 (6-8), [inc in next st, p 9] 3 times, inc in next st, p 4 (6-8). 43 (47-51) sts. Change to larger needles and working in st st work patt from Chart No 1.
▦ *1st row* K 1 **B**, * 3 **E**, 1 **B**; rep from * to last 2 sts, 2 **E**.
▦ *2nd row* P 1 **E**, * 3 **B**, 1 **E**; rep from * to last 2 sts, 2 **B**.

▦ *3rd row* K in **B**.
▦ *4th row* P in **H**.
▦ *5th row* K 4 **H**, * 1 **G**, 5 **H**; rep from * to last 3 (1-5) sts, 1 **G**, 2 (0-4) **H**. Cont in patt from this chart; always begin each k row at right-hand edge of chart. As the various patts have different numbers of sts for the patt rep they will end at different positions on the chart so make a note of the position where the k row ends and begin the p row at same position. Cont in patt without shaping until 46 (50-54) rows have been worked.
▦ **Neck Shaping** For 1st and 2nd sizes work rem rows in patt; for 3rd size work in **A**.
▦ *Next row* K 12 (13-14) and leave these sts for right back, cast off next 19 (21-23) sts, k to end. Cont on 12 (13-14) sts now rem at end of needle for left back; p 1 row then cast off sts for shoulder edge. Rejoin yarn to neck edge of right back sts, p to end. Cast off these sts.

▦ **Front** Work as for back until 29th row of chart has been worked, then make front opening.
▦ *30th row* Using **A**, p 20 (22-24) and leave these sts of right front on a spare needle, cast off 3, p to end. Cont on 20 (22-24) sts now rem on needle for left front taking care to keep patt correct. Work 11 (15-19) rows thus ending at the opening edge.
▦ **Neck Shaping** Cast off 4 (5-6) sts at beg of next row, 2 sts at same edge on next alt row and 1 st on next 2 alt rows; you have now worked a total of 48 (52-56) rows in patt, reaching same position as on back. Cast off rem 12 (13-14) sts for shoulder edge. With right side facing rejoin yarn to sts of right front and cont in patt for 10 (14-18) rows thus ending at the opening edge. Work neck shaping as for left front, p 1 row on rem 12 (13-14) sts then cast off.

▦ **Sleeves** With smaller needles and **E** cast on 23 (27-29) sts and work as for back welt from ** to **.
▦ *Inc row* P 2 (4-2), [inc in next st,

p 5 (5-4)] 3 (3-5) times, inc in next st, p 2 (4-1). 27 (31-35) sts. Change to larger needles and working in st st work patt from Chart No 2; on the first 4 rows the patt will fit in same way as on back. Cont in patt and inc 1 st at both ends of next row, then every foll 6th row 1 (2-3) times, then every foll 4th row 4 (3-2) times, working extra sts into patt. Cont on 39 (43-47) sts until 33 (35-37) rows have been worked in patt. Cast off all sts.

▦ **Front Borders** With right side of work facing and using smaller needles and **A**, pick up and k 13 (17-21) sts along front edge of right front and work in rib beg with 2nd row. If sweater is for a boy work 4 rows in rib then cast off in rib. If for a girl work 1 row then make buttonholes.

▦ *Next row* Beg at lower edge, right side facing, rib 3 (5-5), yrn, p 2 tog, rib 4 (6-10), yrn, p 2 tog, rib 2. Work 2 more rows in rib then cast off in rib. Pick up same number of sts along front edge of left front. If sweater is for a girl work 4 rows in rib beg with 2nd row then cast off in rib. If for a boy rep 2nd rib row then make buttonholes.

▦ *Next row* Beg at upper edge, right side facing, rib 2, p 2 tog, yrn, rib 4 (6-10), p 2 tog, yrn, rib 3 (5-5). Rib 2 more rows then cast off in rib.

▦ **Finishing and Collar** Join shoulder seams. With right side of work facing and using smaller needles and **G**, beg half-way across right front border pick up and k 14 (15-16) sts along right front neck edge, 25 (27-29) sts across back neck and 14 (15-16) sts along left front neck edge ending half-way across left front border. Beg with 1st row as this is right side of collar, work 5(5.5-6) cm, 2(2⅛-2⅜)in, in rib then cast off loosely in rib.

▦ On each side edge mark a point 10.5(12-13)cm, 4⅛(4¾-5⅛in), down from shoulder seam for armholes and sew cast-off edge of sleeves between markers. Join side and sleeve seams.

▦ Slip-st edges of front borders

to base of opening overlapping buttonhole border on the button border. Sew on buttons to correspond with buttonholes.

STYLE 2

▦ **Back** With smaller needles and **E** cast on 39 (43-47) sts and work as given for Style 1 until the inc row has been worked. Change to larger needles and working in st st work patt from Chart No 3.

▦ *1st row* K 3 **E**, * 1 **B**, 3 **E**; rep from * to end.

▦ *2nd row* P 1 **B**, * 1 **E**, 3 **B**; rep from * to last 2 sts, 1 **E**, 1 **B**.

▦ *3rd row* K in **B**.

▦ *4th row* P in **H**. Now begin the bird motifs arranged as foll:

▦ *5th row* K 5 (7-9) **H**, * 2 **G**, 1 **H**, 2 **G**, 11 **H**; * rep from * to * once, 2 **G**, 1 **H**, 2 **G**, 1 (3-5) **H**. Cont as now set until motifs are completed then cont working from chart; begin each k row at right-hand edge of chart and mark on chart the position where rows end so that p row can begin at same position. Cont without shaping until 46 (50-54) rows have been worked in patt. Working rem rows in patt work neck shaping as for Style 1.

▦ **Front** Work as for back until 29th row of chart has been worked. Cont in patt and work front opening on foll row, as given for Style 1; cont working correct patt from Chart No 3 and complete as for front of Style 1.

▦ **Sleeves** With smaller needles and **E** cast on 23 (27-29) sts and work as for sleeves of Style 1 until the inc row has been worked. Change to larger needles and working in st st work patt from Chart No 3, working as for back until 4th row has been worked.

▦ Work 5th row as on back but working the sts from * to * once. Cont in patt but inc 1 st at both ends of next row, then every foll 6th row 1 (2-3) times then every foll 4th row 4 (3-2) times working extra sts into patt. Cont on 39 (43-47) sts until 33 (35-37) rows have been worked in patt. Cast off all sts.

▦ **Front Borders** Work front borders as for Style 1 but using **D**, work collar as for Style 1 but using **A**, make up as for Style 1.

STYLE 3

▦ **Back** With smaller needles and **C** cast on 39 (43-47) sts and work as given for Style 1 until the inc row has been worked. Change to larger needles and working in st st work patt from Chart No 4.

▦ *1st row* K 1 **C**, * 1 **B**, 1 **C**; rep from * to end.

▦ *2nd row* P in **B**.

▦ *3rd row* * K 2 **B**, 1 **G**; rep from * to last 1 (2-0) sts, 1 (2-0) **B**.

▦ *4th row* P 1 (2-0) **G**, * 1 **B**, 2 **G**; rep from * to end. Cont in patt as now set always beg each k row at right-hand edge of chart and mark the position where row ends then begin p row at this position.

▦ Cont without shaping until 46 (50-54) rows have been worked from chart then work neck

shaping as for Style 1 but working in patt.

▦ **Front** Work as for back until 29th row of chart has been worked. Using **B**, work front opening as for Style 1 and cont working correct patt; complete as for front of Style 1.

▦ **Sleeves** With smaller needles and **C** cast on 23 (27-29) sts and work as for sleeves of Style 1 until the inc row has been worked. Change to larger needles and working in st st work patt from Chart No 4.

▦ *1st row* K 1 **C**, * 1 **B**, 1 **C**; rep from * to end.

▦ *2nd row* P in **B**.

▦ *3rd row* * K 2 **B**, 1 **G**; rep from * to last 0 (1-2) sts, k 0 (1-2) **B**.

▦ *4th row* P 0 (1-2) **G**, * 1 **B**, 2 **G**; rep from * to end. Cont working from this chart and complete as for sleeves of Style 1. Work front borders as for Style 1 but using **D**, work collar as for Style 1 but using **C**, make up as for Style 1.

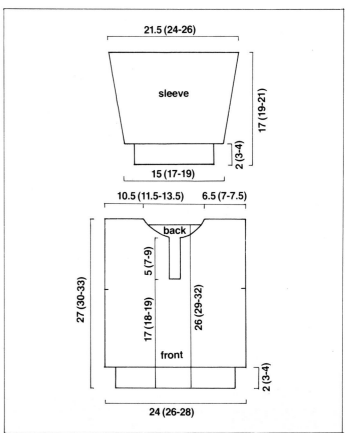

On each chart begin reading knit rows from right-hand edge; as the various patt panels have a different number of sts in the patt repeat they will end at different positions on the chart so mark where the knit row ends and begin the purl row at this position. For Style 2 the bird arrangement is explained in the instructions.

KEY

F
A
E
D
G
B
H
C

1

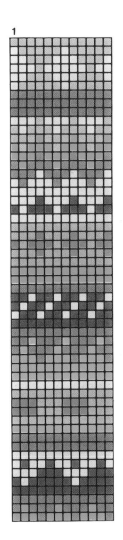

2

3

4

SLEEPY PIXIE LAYETTE

One of the delights of knitting for babies is that you can sometimes enjoy pampering them with luxurious yarns, like the soft alpaca blend yarn used here. This heart-melting pixie with the mischievous eyes can happily be taken on an outing when the temperature drops. Indoors you can take off his edge-to-edge cardigan and his long pixie hat to reveal a cable sweater with front opening.

CHECKLIST

Materials

*Alpaca blend double knit: for cardigan, 2(3-3) × 50g balls grey (**A**) and 2 (3-3) balls turquoise blue (**B**); for sweater, 3 balls (all sizes) grey; for hat, 2 balls (all sizes) turquoise blue, and for socks, one ball turquoise blue. 4-ply yarn for the trousers: 3 × 50g balls (all sizes) sky blue (**C**). Pair each of needles size 3mm, 3¼mm and 3¾mm; two double-pointed needles size 4mm for cardigan; a cable needle; 3 buttons for sweater; elastic thread for trousers.*

Sizes

Three sizes, to fit ages 3 (6-9) months. Actual measurements of cardigan, sweater and trousers shown on diagram. Socks, in one size only, fit a baby up to 6 months.

Stitches used

Two-colour patt, worked on double-pointed needles as foll:
*1st row (right side) With **A**, k 1, * slip 1 pw keeping yarn at back, k 1; rep from * to end. Return to opposite edge of work.*
*2nd row (right side) With **B**, p 1, * k 1, p 1; rep from * to end.*
*3rd row (wrong side) With **A**, slip 1 pw, * p 1, then slip 1 pw keeping yarn at front; rep from * to end. Return to opposite edge.*
*4th row (wrong side) With **B**, p 1, * k 1, p 1; rep from * to end.*
These 4 rows form one patt.
Cable 4 back = slip next 2 sts on cable needle, leave at back, k 2, then k 2 from cable needle. For arrangement of cables on each design see instructions.

Tensions

*Over two-colour patt using 4mm needles, 23 sts and 46 rows to 10cm (4in). Work a sample on 29 sts casting on with **B**; k 1 row then work in patt as given above; it is essential to work a sample of this patt so that you become familiar with it before beg garment. Over cable patt on sweater using 3¾mm needles, 34 sts and 34 rows to 10cm (4in); work a sample on 40 sts as given for 1st size on back. Over double rib using 4-ply yarn and 3¼mm needles, 34 sts and 34 rows measured unstretched to 10cm (4in). Work a sample on 38 sts.*

INSTRUCTIONS

CARDIGAN

▦ **Back** With double-pointed 4mm needles and **B** cast on 57 (63-69) sts and k 1 row. Join on **A** and work in two-colour patt. Cont without shaping until work measures 23(26-29)cm, 9(10¼- 11⅜)in, from beg, ending with a 4th patt row.
▦ **Neck Shaping** *1st row* Patt 20 (22-24) and leave these sts of right back on a spare needle, cast off next 17 (19-21) sts loosely, patt to end. Cont on 20 (22-24) sts now rem on needle for left back; keep patt correct changing ends as usual. Dec 1 st at neck

edge on next 2 rows then at same edge on next alt row. Work 1 row then cast off rem 17 (19-21) sts for shoulder edge. Rejoin yarn to sts of right back at outer edge in order to work 2nd patt row; complete as for left back reversing shapings.

◾ **Right Front** With double-pointed 4mm needles and **B** cast on 29 (33-37) sts and k 1 row. Join on **A** and work in patt. Cont without shaping until work

measures 20.5(23.5-26.5)cm, 8(9¼-10½)in, from beg, ending with a 4th patt row. **

◾ **Neck Shaping** *1st row* Cast off 6 (7-8), patt to end. Keeping patt correct dec 1 st at neck edge on next 2 (3-4) rows then at same edge on next 4 alt rows. Cont on rem 17 (19-21) sts until work matches back to shoulder edge. Cast off loosely.

◾ **Left Front** Work as for right front to **.

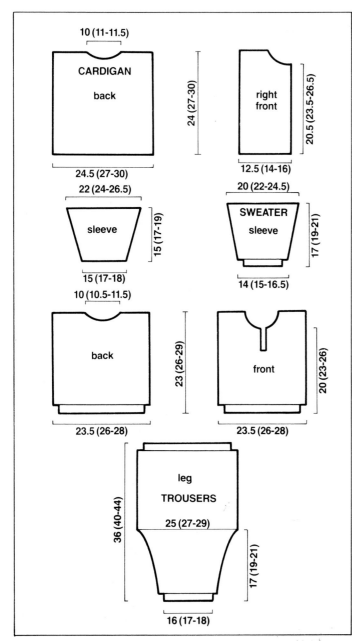

◾ **Neck Shaping** *1st row* Patt 23 (26-29) then cast off rem 6 (7-8) sts and fasten off. Return to opposite edge in order to work 2nd patt row and complete as for right front reversing shapings.

◾ **Sleeves** With double-pointed 4mm needles and **B** cast on 35 (39-41) sts and k 1 row. Join on **A** and work in patt. Inc 1 st at both ends of every foll 8th row 6 (8-10) times, then every foll 6th row twice for 1st size only, working extra sts into patt. Cont on 51 (55-61) sts until work measures 15 (17-19)cm, 5⅞(6¾-7½)in, from beg, ending with a 2nd or 4th patt row. Cast off loosely.

◾ **Front Facings** With right side of work facing and using 3¼mm needles and **B**, pick up and k 63 (72-81) sts along front edge of right front. K 1 row on wrong side then beg with another k row work 3 rows in st st. Cast off. Work similar facing on left front.

◾ **Finishing and Neck Edging** Join shoulder seams. With right side facing and using 3¼mm needles and **B**, pick up and k 20 (22-24) sts along right front neck edge leaving facing free, then 21 (23-25) sts across back neck and 20 (22-24) sts along left front neck edge leaving facing free. K 1 row then cast off. On each side edge mark a point 11(12-13)cm, 4¼(4¾-5⅛)in, down from shoulder seam for armholes and sew cast-off edge of sleeves between marked points. Join side and sleeve seams. Fold in facings along front edges to wrong side and slip-st in place.

SWEATER

◾ **Back** With 3mm needles cast on 69 (75-83) sts and work in single rib.
◾ *1st row* (right side) P 1, * k 1, p 1; rep from * to end.
◾ *2nd row* K 1, * p 1, k 1; rep from * to end. Rep these 2 rows twice more then 1st row again.
◾ *Inc row* Rib 4 (1-5), [inc in next st, rib 5] 10 (12-12) times, inc in next st, rib 4 (1-5). 80 (88-96) sts.

Change to 3¾mm needles and work in cable patt.
◾ *1st row* P 6 (2-6), * k 4, p 4; * rep from * to * ending k 4, p 6 (2-6).
◾ *2nd row* K 6 (2-6), * p 4, k 4; * rep from * to * ending p 4, k 6 (2-6). Rep these 2 rows once.
◾ *5th row* P 6 (2-6), * cable 4 back, p 4; * rep from * to * ending cable 4 back, p 6 (2-6).
◾ *6th to 8th rows* Rep 2nd row once then 1st and 2nd rows again. These 8 rows form one patt. Cont in patt until work measures 22(25-28)cm, 8⅝(9¾-11)in, from beg, ending with a wrong-side row.
◾ **Neck Shaping** *Next row* Patt 28 (31-33) and leave these sts of right back on needle, cast off next 24 (26-30) sts, patt to end. Cont on 28 (31-33) sts now rem at end of needle for left back. Dec 1 st at neck edge on next row, cast off 4 sts at beg of foll row then work 1 row without shaping. Cast off rem 23 (26-28) sts for shoulder edge. Rejoin yarn to neck edge of right back sts, cast off 4, patt to end. Dec 1 st at neck edge on next row, work 1 row then cast off rem 23 (26-28) sts.

◾ **Front** Work as for back until front measures 14(16-18)cm, 5½(6¼-7⅛)in, from beg, ending with a wrong-side row.
◾ **Front Opening** *Next row* Patt 38 (42-46) and leave these sts of left front on a spare needle, cast off next 4 sts, patt to end. Cont on 38 (42-46) sts now rem on needle for right front, without shaping, until work measures 20(23-26)cm, 7⅞(9-10¼)in, from beg, ending at the opening edge.
◾ **Neck Shaping** Cast off 8 (9-11) sts at beg of next row, 3 sts at same edge on next alt row, 2 sts on next alt row and 1 st on next 2 alt rows. Work 1 row on rem 23 (26-28) sts then cast off for shoulder edge. Rejoin yarn with wrong side facing to sts of left front and cont in patt until you have worked 1 row fewer than on right front to beg of neck. Work neck shaping as for right front and after last dec row work 2 rows straight then cast off rem 23 (26-28) sts.

Sleeves With 3mm needles cast on 37 (39-43) sts and work 7 rows in rib as on back welt.

Inc row Rib 3 (1-3), [inc in next st, rib 2] 10 (12-12) times, inc in next st, rib 3 (1-3). 48 (52-56) sts. Change to 3¾mm needles and patt.

1st row P 2 (4-2), * k 4 to form a cable, p 4; * rep from * to * ending k 4 to form a cable, p 2 (4-2). Cont in patt as now set for 4 more rows, then inc 1 st at both ends of next row, then every foll 6th row 2 (1-0) times, then every foll 4th row 7 (10-13) times, working extra sts into cable patt. Cont on 68 (76-84) sts until work measures 17 (19-21)cm, 6¾ (7½-8¼)in, from beg. Cast off.

Finishing and Borders Join shoulder seams matching patt. With right side of work facing and using 3mm needles, pick up and k 15 (16-18) sts along right front neck edge, 31 (33-37) sts across back neck and 15 (16-18) sts along left front neck edge. 61 (65-73) sts. Beg with 2nd row work in rib for 5 rows then cast off loosely in rib. If sweater is for a boy, with right side facing and using 3mm needles, pick up and k 29 (33-37) sts along left front edge of opening including edge of neck border. Beg with 2nd row work in rib and after working 2 rows make buttonholes.

Next row Beg at lower edge, wrong side facing, rib 8, [yrn, p 2 tog, rib 6 (8-10) twice, yrn, p 2 tog, rib 3. Work 2 more rows in rib then cast off in rib. Work similar border on right front omitting buttonholes. If sweater is for a girl the buttonholes should be made in right front border; the row begins at neck edge and should be read in reverse.

On each side edge mark a point 10 (11-12)cm, 4 (4¼-4¾)in, down from shoulder seam for armholes and sew cast-off edge of sleeves between marked points. Join side and sleeve seams. Sew lower edges of front borders to base of opening, overlapping buttonhole border on the other border. Sew on buttons to correspond.

TROUSERS

Right Leg With 3mm needles and **C** cast on 45 (49-53) sts and work in single rib as given for sweater welt for 7 rows.

Inc row Rib 2 (4-6), [inc in next st, rib 3] 10 times, inc in next st, rib 2 (4-6). 56 (60-64) sts. Change to 3¼mm needles and work in double rib (cable at centre front).

1st row P 2 (0-2), [k 2, p 2] 2 (3-3) times, k 4 for a cable, [p 2, k 2] 10 (11-11) times, p 2 (0-2).

2nd row K 2 (0-2), [p 2, k 2] 10 (11-11) times, p 4, [k 2, p 2] 2 (3-3) times, k 2 (0-2). Rep these 2 rows twice more.

7th row Rib 10 (12-14), cable 4 back, rib 42 (44-46).

8th row As 2nd. These 8 rows form one patt. ** Cont in patt but inc 1 st at both ends of next row, then every foll 4th row 7 (9-11) times then every alt row 6 times, then cast on 2 sts at beg of next 2 rows, working extra sts at sides in double rib. Work 1 row on these 88 (96-104) sts thus ending with a 4th patt row. For all sizes there is a p 2 rib at beg and end of right-side rows. ** Cut yarn and leave sts on a spare needle.

Left Leg Work as for right leg for first 8 rows then change to 3¼mm needles and patt which is the reverse of right leg.

1st row P 2 (0-2), [k 2, p 2] 10 (11-11) times, k 4 for a cable, [p 2, k 2] 2 (3-3) times, p 2 (0-2). Cont in patt as now set until 8th row has been worked then cont as for right leg from ** to **. Join legs.

5th row of patt Cast on 1 and k this st, [p 2, k 2] 14 (15-16) times, p 2, k 4, [p 2, k 2] 6 (7-8) times, p 2, turn and cast on 2 sts, turn, then working sts of right leg [p 2, k 2] 6 (7-8) times, p 2, k 4, [p 2, k 2] 14 (15-16) times, p 2, turn and cast on 1 st. 180 (196-212) sts. Cont in patt as now set across all sts until work measures 34 (38-42)cm, 13⅜ (15-16½)in, from beg, ending with a right-side row.

Dec row For 1st size p 4, [p 2 tog, p 6, p 2 tog, p 7] 10 times, p 2 tog, p 4 (for 2nd size p 1, [p 2 tog, p 6] 24 times, p 2 tog, p 1; for 3rd size p 7, [p 2 tog, p 5] 29 times, p rem 2 sts).

All sizes Cont on rem 159 (171-183) sts; change to 3mm needles and work 8 rows in single rib. Cast off in rib.

Finishing Join inner leg seams. Join centre back seam. Insert 3 rows of elastic thread through waistband on wrong side securing ends in back seam.

HAT

With 3mm needles cast on 105 (113-123) sts and work in rib as on sweater for 8 rows but working 1 inc in centre of last row. Change to 3¼mm needles and work in patt on 106 (114-124) sts.

1st row P 9 (9-10), * k 4, p 17 (19-21); * rep from * to * 3 times more, k 4, p 9 (9-10).

2nd row K 9 (9-10), * p 4, k 17 (19-21); * rep from * to * 3 times more, p 4, k 9 (9-10). Rep these 2 rows twice more.

7th row P 9 (9-10), * cable 4 back, p 17 (19-21); * rep from * to * 3 times more, cable 4 back, p 9 (9-10).

8th row As 2nd. These 8 rows form one patt. Cont in patt until work measures 12cm (4¾in) from beg, ending with a right-side row, then begin shaping.

1st dec row K 7 (7-8), k 2 tog, * p 4, SKPO, k 13 (15-17), k 2 tog; * rep from * to * 3 times more, p 4, SKPO, k 7 (7-8). 96 (104-114) sts. Work 9 rows in patt having 8 (8-9) sts in rev st st at each side and 15 (17-19) sts between cables.

2nd dec row K 6 (6-7), k 2 tog, * p 4, SKPO, k 11 (13-15), k 2 tog; * rep from * to * 3 times more, p 4, SKPO, k 6 (6-7). 86 (94-104) sts. Cont working decs before and after the cables on every foll 10th row 5 (5-6) times more. Work 9 rows on rem 36 (44-44) sts.

For 1st size only, cont as foll:

** *Next row* K 2 tog, * p 4, SKTPO;* rep from * to * 3 times more, p 4, k 2 tog. Work 9 rows on rem 36 sts.

Next row P 1, [p 3 tog, p 2 tog] 5 times. Cut yarn, thread end through rem sts, draw up but do not close yet.

For 2nd and 3rd sizes, cont as foll:

Next row K 2, * p 4, SKPO, k 1, k 2 tog; * rep from * to * 3 times more, p 4, k 2. Work 9 rows on rem 26 sts then complete as for 1st size from ** to end.

Finishing Make large tassel and sew the end of yarn at top of hat firmly to top of tassel. Backstitch seam of hat.

SOCKS

Beg at upper edge cast on 48 sts using 3mm needles and work in patt.

1st row [K 1, p 1] 11 times, k 4, [p 1, k 1] 11 times.

2nd row [P 1, k 1] 11 times, p 4, [k 1, p 1] 11 times. Rep these 2 rows twice more.

7th row Rib 22, cable 4 back, rib 22.

8th row As 2nd. These 8 rows form one patt. Cont in patt until work measures 9cm (3½in) from beg, ending with a wrong-side row then divide for heel.

Next row Cut yarn, slip 13 sts onto a holder, rejoin yarn, rib 9, work the 4 sts of cable, rib 9, turn and place rem 13 sts on a holder. Cont on centre 22 sts for instep keeping cable correct and work 5cm (2in) ending with a wrong-side row. Cut yarn.

With right side facing rejoin yarn to first group of 13 sts at side, rib these sts, pick up and k 20 sts along side of instep, then working sts of instep p 2 tog, k 2 tog, [p 1, k 1] 3 times, p 2 tog, [k 1, p 1] 3 times, k 2 tog, p 2 tog, then pick up and k 20 sts along other side of instep, then rib 13 sts at other side of heel. Cont on these 83 sts working in rib across all sts for 9 rows then shape toe as foll:

1st row P 2 tog, rib 38, k 3 tog, rib 38, p 2 tog.

2nd row K 1, * p 1, k 1; rep from * to end.

3rd row K 2 tog, rib 36, p 3 tog, rib 36, k 2 tog.

4th row P 1, * k 1, p 1; rep from * to end. Cont to dec 1 st at each end and work double dec in centre on next row and next 3 alt rows. Cast off rem 59 sts. Fold this edge in half and sew. Join seam under foot and along leg.

STRAWBERRY RIPE

Lyrically charming and as fresh and innocent as a nursery rhyme, this little set in soft cotton includes two jackets, one embroidered with a cherry motif and one with strawberries, each with bootees to match. The cherry jacket, knitted in a ridge pattern, fastens at the front, while the strawberry jacket is knitted in reverse stocking stitch and fastens at the back, though both jackets are knitted to the same basic style and can be worn the other way around. Both jackets have a garter stitch lower border and a tubular neck border through which a crocheted or twisted silk cord is threaded.

CHECKLIST

Materials

Pingouin Corrida 3: 6 × 50g balls cream – 2 for each jacket and one for each pair of bootees.
DMC coton perlé for the embroidery: for the cherry jacket and bootees, one skein each of 321, 816, 950 and 993; for the strawberry jacket and bootees, one skein each of 350, 352, 816, 817, 891 and 993.
Pair of needles size 3mm; 16 buttons – 6 for each jacket and 2 for each pair of bootees.

Sizes

Jackets are in three sizes to fit ages 3 (6-9 months). Bootees are in one size to fit a baby up to 6 months.

Stitches used

For the cherry jacket: g st; st st, patt, worked on any number of sts as foll: beg with a k row work 5 rows in st st.
 6th row (wrong side) K all sts. These 6 rows form one patt.
 Tubular rib, for neck border, as foll:
 1st row * K 1, yarn to front, slip 1 pw, yarn to back;* rep from* to*.
  All rows are alike and work forms a tube with an opening at the ends through which a cord can be passed.
For the strawberry jacket: g st; st st; rev st st; tubular rib as for cherry jacket.

Tension

For both jackets (cherry jacket over patt, strawberry jacket over rev st st), using 3mm needles, 28 sts and 40 rows to 10cm (4in). Work a sample on 34 sts. It is also advisable to work a sample of tubular rib in order to become familiar with it: cast on an even number of sts and k 1 row then work as given above.

INSTRUCTIONS

CHERRY JACKET

Main Part This is worked in one piece from side to side. Beg with left front cast on 40 (46-52) sts and work at once in patt; front border is worked later. Cont until 36 (42-48) rows have been worked then work 4 rows in st st.
 ** 5th row of patt K 30 (34-38) and leave these sts of main part on a holder, k rem 10 (12-14) sts.
 6th row K 10 (12-14), turn and cast on 30 (34-38) sts for left sleeve. Cont in patt on these 40 (46-52) sts and work 11 (13-15) complete patts then work 4 rows in st st.

and cherry sweet

STRAWBERRY MOTIFS

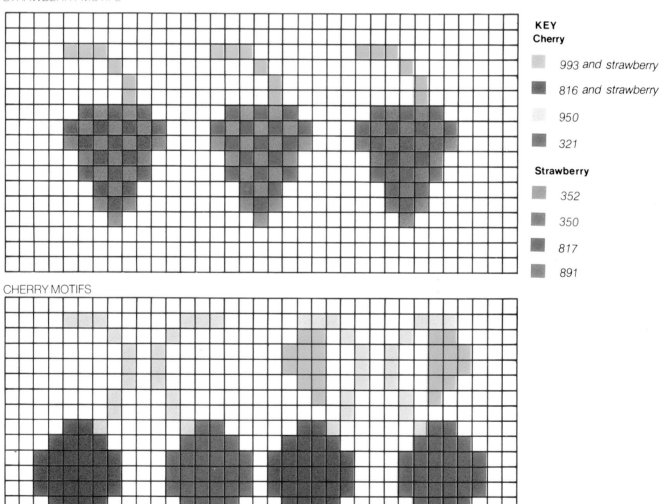

KEY
Cherry

993 and strawberry

816 and strawberry

950

321

Strawberry

352

350

817

891

CHERRY MOTIFS

▥ *5th row of patt* Cast off 30 (34-38) sts to complete sleeve, k to end.

▥ *6th row* K 10 (12-14), then onto same needle k the 30 (34-38) sts of main part which were left on a holder. ✲✲ Cont on 40 (46-52) sts for back and work 13 (15-17) patts then work 4 rows in st st. Now work right sleeve as for left sleeve from ✲✲ to ✲✲. Cont on 40 (46-52) sts which are now on needle for right front and work 6 (7-8) complete patts then work 5 rows in st st. Cast off.

▥ **Yoke** With right side facing pick up and k 21 (24-27) sts along upper edge of right front, 36 (42-48) sts across top of right sleeve, 41 (47-53) sts across top of back, 36 (42-48) sts across top of left sleeve and 21 (24-27) sts across top of left front. 155 (179-203) sts. K 1 row on wrong side. Now work in st st beg with another k row; work 2 rows then begin shaping.

▥ *3rd row* K 5, [k 2 tog, k 10] 12 (14-16) times, k 2 tog, k 4. Cont on rem 142 (164-186) sts and work 3 rows in st st. Note that decs are not intended to form lines but have a random effect.

▥ *7th row* K 10, [k 2 tog, k 9] 12 (14-16) times. Cont on rem 130 (150-170) sts and work 3 rows in st st.

▥ *11th row* K 2, [k 2 tog, k 8] 12 (14-16) times, k 2 tog, k 6. Cont on rem 117 (135-153) sts and work 3 rows in st st.

▥ *15th row* K 5, [k 2 tog, k 7] 11 (13-15) times, k 2 tog, k 11. Cont on rem 105 (121-137) sts and work 3 rows in st st.

▥ *19th row* K 3 (4-5), [k 2 tog, k 5] 14 (16-18) times, k 2 tog, k 2 (3-4). P 1 row on rem 90 (104-118) sts then work in tubular rib for 12 rows. Cast off in k.

▥ **Borders** With right side facing pick up and k 60 (66-72) sts along front edge of right front including yoke, working into the upper side of the tubular rib section leaving the underside free. Work in g st and after working 3 rows make buttonholes.

▥ *4th row* Beg at lower edge k 4, [yfd, k 2 tog, k 7 (8-9)] 6 times, k 2.

Work 2 more rows in g st then cast off loosely. Work border on left front in same way but working into underside of tubular rib section and omitting buttonholes.

▥ With right side facing pick up and k 104 (120-136) sts all around lower edge of jacket. Work 6 rows in g st then cast off loosely. With right side facing pick up and k 36 (40-44) sts along lower edge of one sleeve; work 6 rows in g st then cast off loosely. Work other cuff in same way. Join sleeve seams. Embroider cherry motifs around yoke using Swiss darning method explained on page 6.

▥ Using 2 strands of ecru and 2 strands of 2 other colours make a twisted cord (see below) about 61(66-71)cm, 26(28-30)in, long and insert this through the tubular rib section at top of yoke to tie at front. Sew on buttons to correspond with buttonholes.

▥ **Twisted Cord** For each length of cord, decide how long you wish the finished cord to be and cut strands of yarn about three times this length, using half the number of strands that the finished cord is to have. Hold the strands with the ends level and, using a separate strand of yarn, tie them tightly together near one end. Slip this tied end over a hook and twist the strands tightly together starting at the other end. When a very tight twist is formed place one finger at the centre and bring the ends together. Remove your finger and the strands will twist into a cord. Tie both ends firmly together and cut off the original tie. An alternative method of making a cord is to make a length of crochet chain, using a large crochet hook and working with several strands of yarn together. For a neater cord, work back along the chain making a row of slip-sts along each side.

Note It is dangerous ever to tighten a cord around a baby's neck, so adjust the tie to a comfortable length for the neck and then sew very securely and firmly at each edge, leaving the

ends loose to tie in a bow.

▥ **Right Bootee** Beg with centre of sole cast on 40 sts and work in g st shaping sides and centre.

▥ *1st row* K.

▥ *2nd row* K 1, yfd, k 18, [yfd, k 1] twice, yfd, k 18, yfd, k 1.

▥ *3rd and alt rows* K but working the yfd loops tbl to avoid a hole.

▥ *4th row* K 2, yfd, k 18, yfd, k 3, yfd, k 2, yfd, k 18, yfd, k 2.

▥ *6th row* K 3, yfd, k 18, [yfd, k 4] twice, yfd, k 18, yfd, k 3.

▥ *8th row* K 4, yfd, k 18, yfd, k 6, yfd, k 5, yfd, k 18, yfd, k 4.

▥ *10th row* K 5, yfd, k 18, [yfd, k 7] twice, yfd, k 18, yfd, k 5.

▥ *12th row* K 24, yfd, k 9, yfd, k 8, yfd, k 24.

▥ *13th row* As 3rd. Cont on these 68 sts and work 11 rows in g st.

▥ **Instep** *1st row* K 38, k 2 tog, turn thus leaving 28 sts unworked.

▥ *2nd row* Slip 1, p 8, p 2 tog, turn. There are 28 sts at this edge also.

▥ *3rd row* Slip 1, k 8, k 2 tog, turn.

▥ *4th row* Slip 1, p 8, p 2 tog, turn. Rep 3rd and 4th rows 8 times more. Turn as usual after last row and k to end on right side of work.

▥ *Next row* K 18, k 2 tog, k 8, k 2 tog, k 18. 46 sts.

▥ *Next row* K 9 and leave these sts on a safety pin, cast off 28, k to end. ✲✲ Cont on last group of 9 sts.

▥ *Next row* K 9, turn and cast on 6 sts for button-strap. Work 3 rows in g st on these 15 sts then cast off. For ankle strap cast on 13 sts, take needle with these sts in right hand and with wrong side facing k the other group of 9 sts. Cont on 22 sts and work 3 rows in g st then cast off. Make a buttonhole loop on end of ankle strap. Embroider a cherry motif on instep. Fold cast-on edge of sole in half and sew with a flat seam. Sew back seam of bootee. Sew on button to button-strap.

▥ **Left Bootee** Work as for right bootee to ✲✲; cont on last group of 9 sts.

▥ *Next row* K 9, turn and cast on 13 sts for ankle strap. Work 3 rows in g st on 22 sts then cast off. For button-strap cast on 6 sts, take needle with these sts in right hand and with wrong side facing k the other group of 9 sts. Work 3 rows in g st on these 15 sts then cast off. Complete as for right bootee.

STRAWBERRY JACKET

▥ **Main Part** This is worked in one piece from side to side. Beg with right back cast on 40 (46-52) sts and work in rev st st for 40 (46-52) rows.

▥ ✲✲ *Next row* P 30 (34-38) and leave these sts of main part on a holder, p rem 10 (12-14) sts.

▥ *Next row* K 10 (12-14), turn and cast on 30 (34-38) sts for right sleeve. Cont in patt on these 40 (46-52) sts and work 70 (82-94) rows.

▥ *Next row* Cast off 30 (34-38) sts to complete sleeve, p to end.

▥ *Next row* K 10 (12-14), then onto same needle k sts of main part which were left on holder. ✲✲ Cont on 40 (46-52) sts for front and work 82 (94-106) rows in rev st st. Now work left sleeve as for right sleeve from ✲✲ to ✲✲. Cont on 40 (46-52) sts which are now on needle for left back and work 41 (47-53) rows in rev st st. Cast off.

▥ **Yoke** Pick up same groups of sts as for cherry jacket along upper edge in foll order, left back, left sleeve, front, right sleeve, right back. Work entire yoke as for cherry jacket.

▥ **Borders** Work border on left back as for right front of cherry jacket and border on right back as for left front. Work all other borders as for cherry jacket.

▥ **Finishing** As for cherry jacket but embroider strawberry motifs on yoke.

▥ **Bootees** Work both bootees as for cherry set but embroider a strawberry motif on each instep with stalk pointing to the outside as shown.

THE YOUNGEST CABIN BOY

Walking already, even if he does sometimes look as though he is having trouble finding his legs on dry land, this young sailor is well equipped with a warm, double-breasted jacket, appropriately enough in an easy-to-work version of the popular favourite, fisherman rib. The jacket has a smart collar and revers, and the trousers have shoulder straps for a comfortable fit and are worked on smaller needles to give extra firmness.

CHECKLIST

Materials

Patons Diploma Gold double knit: 6 (7-8) × 50g balls dark blue for jacket and 6 (7-8) balls red for trousers.
Pair each of needles size 3¼mm, 3¾mm and 4mm; 4 buttons for jacket and 2 for trousers.

Sizes

Three sizes to fit ages 12 months (18 months–2 years). Actual measurements shown on diagram.

Stitches used

Single rib; single-sided fisherman rib, *worked on an odd number of sts as foll:*

> 1st row *(right side) K 1, * k next st but in row below, inserting needle through work and allowing st above to drop off needle, p 1; rep from * to last 2 sts, k 1 below as before, k 1.*
> 2nd row *K 1, * p 1, k 1; rep from * to end. These 2 rows form patt.*
> *When casting off over this patt it should be done loosely in normal single rib as sts appear.*

Tension

Over patt using 4mm needles, 21 sts and 44 rows to 10cm (4in); work a sample on 25 sts. Over patt using 3¾mm needles, 22 sts and 48 rows to 10cm (4in); work a sample on 27 sts. When counting rows, each k rib showing on right side counts as 2 rows.

INSTRUCTIONS

JACKET

Back With 3¾mm needles, cast on 63 (67-71) sts and work in single rib.

1st row (right side) P 1, * k 1, p 1; rep from * to end.

2nd row K 1, * p 1, k 1; rep from * to end. Rep these 2 rows once. Change to 4mm needles and work in patt as given above. Cont until work measures 16(18-20)cm, 6¼(7⅛-7⅞)in, from beg, ending with a wrong-side row.

Armhole Shaping Cast off 3 sts at beg of next 2 rows, 2 sts at beg of next 2 rows and 1 st at beg of next 2 rows.

Cont on rem 51 (55-59) sts until work measures 28(31-34)cm, 11(12¼-13⅜)in, from beg, ending with a wrong-side row.

Shoulder Shaping Cast off 5 (5-6) sts at beg of next 4 rows and 6 (7-6) sts at beg of next 2 rows. Cast off rem 19 (21-23) sts for back neck.

Right Front With 3¾mm needles cast on 41 (43-45) sts and work 4 rows in single rib as on back then change to 4mm needles and work in patt. Cont until work matches back to armhole but ending with a right-side row.

▦ **Armhole and Front Shaping** Cast off 3 sts at beg of next row, 2 sts at same edge on next alt row and 1 st on next alt row; work 4 rows on rem 35 (37-39) sts thus ending at front edge. Dec 1 st at beg of next row and next 18 (19-20) alt rows then cont on rem 16 (17-18) sts until work matches back to beg of shoulder, ending at side edge.

▦ **Shoulder Shaping** Cast off 5 (5-6) sts at beg of next row and next alt row, work 1 row then cast off rem 6 (7-6) sts.

▦ **Left Front** Work as for right front until work measures 5(6-7)cm, 2(2⅜-2¾)in, from beg, ending with a right-side row, then make buttonholes.
▦ *Next row* Rib 4 sts, cast off 2, rib until there are 8 sts on right needle after previous buttonhole, cast off 2, rib to end. On foll row cast on 2 sts over each buttonhole. Cont until work measures 13(15-17)cm, 5⅛(5⅞-6¾)in, from beg, ending with a right-side row, then make 2 more buttonholes in same positions as before. Complete as for right front reversing all shapings.

▦ **Sleeves** With 3¾mm needles cast on 31 (35-39) sts and work 4 rows in rib as on back then change to 4mm needles and work in patt. Inc 1 st at both ends of every foll 8th row 1 (5-9) times, then every foll 6th row 9 (5-1) times. Work extra sts into patt but do not k below on border st at sides. Cont on 51 (55-59) sts until work measures 18(20-22)cm, 7⅛(7⅞-8⅝)in, from beg.
▦ **Top Shaping** Cast off 3 sts at beg of next 2 rows, 2 sts at beg of next 2 rows, 1 st at beg of next 10 (8-6) rows, 2 sts at beg of next 6 (8-10) rows and 4 sts at beg of next 2 rows. Cast off rem 11 (13-15) sts.

▦ **Revers** For right front revers cast on 3 sts using 3¾mm needles and work in single rib shaping inner edge.
▦ *1st row* P 1, k 1, p 1.
▦ *2nd row* K 1, p 1, inc in last st. Cont to inc at this edge on every alt row 12 (13-14) times more. Cast off these 16 (17-18) sts loosely in rib. Work left front revers in same way but reversing shapings.

▦ **Collar** With 3¾mm needles cast on 49 (53-57) sts and work in single rib as given at lower edge of back for 14 (16-18) rows then cast off loosely in rib.

▦ **Finishing** Join shoulder seams matching patt ribs. Sew in sleeves then join side and sleeve seams. With right side of revers to wrong side of fronts, join shaped edges of revers to front shapings, making a flat join. With right side of collar to wrong side of jacket sew cast-on edge to back neck edges and front edges above the end of revers. Sew on buttons to correspond with buttonholes. Turn back collar and revers onto right side.

TROUSERS

▦ **Front** With 3¼mm needles cast on 27 (29-31) sts for one leg. Work 2 rows in single rib as given for jacket then change to 3¾mm needles and work in patt; inc 1 st at both ends of every foll 20th row 4 times then cont on 35 (37-39) sts until work measures 22(24-27)cm, 8⅝(9½-10⅝)in, from beg, ending with a 2nd patt row. ✳✳
Cut yarn and leave sts on a spare needle. Work second leg in same way to ✳✳.
▦ *Next row* Patt 34 (36-38), p rem st tog with 1st st of first leg, patt 34 (36-38) sts of first leg. Cont in patt on these 69 (73-77) sts until work measures 38(42-47)cm, 15(16½-18½)in from beg, ending with a 2nd patt row. Change to 3¼mm needles and work in single rib; work 2 rows then make buttonholes.
▦ *3rd row* Rib 20 (22-22), cast off 2, rib until there are 25 (25-29) sts on right needle after previous buttonhole, cast off 2, rib to end. On foll row cast on 2 sts over each buttonhole. Rib 2 more rows then cast off loosely in rib.

▦ **Back** Work as for front omitting buttonholes in waistband; after working the 6 rows in rib make shoulder straps:
▦ *Next row* Cast off 18 (20-20) sts in rib, rib until there are 7 sts on right needle, leave these on a safety pin for right shoulder strap, cast off next 19 (19-23) sts in rib, rib until there are 7 sts on right needle, leave these on needle for left shoulder strap, cast off rem 18 (20-20) sts in rib and fasten off. Rejoin yarn with wrong side facing to sts of left shoulder strap.
▦ *Next row* [K 1, p 1] 3 times, k 1.
▦ *Next row* K 2, [p 1, k 1] twice, k 1. Rep these 2 rows until strap measures 31(35-39)cm, 12¼(13¾-15⅜)in, from beg. Cast off in rib. Work right shoulder strap in same way.

▦ **Finishing** Join side and inner leg seams. Sew buttons to shoulder straps to match buttonholes.

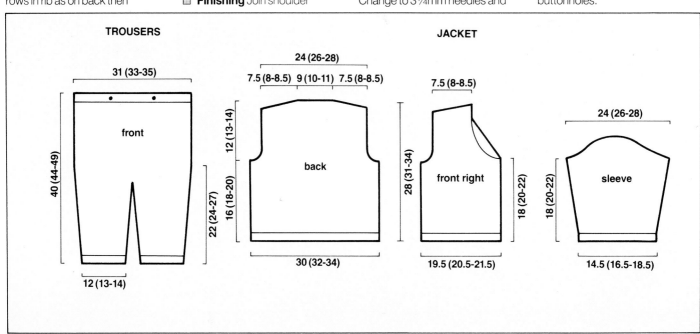

PASTEL PERFECTION

A patchwork blanket as soft as a dream and an elegant two-piece to match: what more could a stylish baby ask for? Knitted in a beautifully soft cotton yarn that is kind and gentle to a delicate skin, the outfit washes easily, dries quickly and is perfect for mild weather wear. The striped top has a wide neckline, with the back lapping over the front so that it slips on and off easily, and the plain, short length pants have an elasticated waist. The blanket, also cotton, is made from 25 separate rectangles, joined with narrow strips of white – perhaps it could be a joint family effort?

CHECKLIST

TWO-PIECE
Materials
Sophie Desroches Coton Mat: for the top, 2 (2-3) × 50g balls peach (A) and one ball white (B); for the trousers, 2 (2-3) balls white. Pair each of needles size 2¼mm, 2¾mm and 3mm; narrow elastic for trousers.

Sizes
Three sizes, to fit ages 6 (9-12) months. Actual measurements shown on diagram.

Stitches used
Double rib; st st.

Tension
Over st st using 3mm needles, 27 sts and 36 rows to 10cm (4in). Work a sample on 32 sts.

INSTRUCTIONS

TOP

▦ **Front** With 2¼mm needles and **B**, cast on 62 (66-74) sts and work in rib.

▦ *1st row* (right side) K 2, * p 2, k 2; rep from * to end.

▦ *2nd row* P 2, * k 2, p 2; rep from * to end. Rep these 2 rows 4 times more then 1st row again.

▦ *12th row* Rib 13 (9-17), [inc in next st, rib 17 (11-19)] 2 (4-2) times, inc in next st, rib 12 (8-16). 65 (71-77) sts. Change to 3mm needles and beg with a k row work in st st working in striped patt of 2 rows **B**, 10 rows **A** throughout. Cont until 50 (54-58) rows have been worked in st st.

▦ **Armhole Shaping** Cast off 3 sts at beg of next 2 rows, 2 sts at beg of next 2 rows and 1 st at beg of next 4 (6-8) rows. Cont on rem 51 (55-59) sts until work measures 21(23-25)cm, 8¼(9-9¾)in, from beg, ending with a p row.

▦ **Neck Shaping** *1st row* K 21 (22-23) and leave these sts of left front on a spare needle, cast off next 9 (11-13) sts, k to end. Cont on 21 (22-23) sts now rem on needle for right front and work 1 row. Cast off 3 (4-4) sts at beg of next row, 2 sts at same edge on next 2 alt rows and 1 st on next alt row; work 3 rows without shaping. ** Dec 1 st at neck edge on next row and next 2 alt rows then dec at same edge on foll 5 rows. Cast off rem 5 (5-6) sts. Rejoin correct colour to neck edge of left front sts, cast off 3 (4-4), p to end. Cast off 2 sts at same edge on next 2 alt rows and 1 st on next alt row then work 4 rows without shaping. Complete as for right front from ** to end.

▦ **Back** Work as for front until armhole shaping is completed then cont until work measures 25(27-29)cm, 9¾(10⅝-11⅜)in, from beg, ending with a p row.

▦ **Neck Shaping** *1st row* K 22 (23-24) and leave these sts of right back on a spare needle, cast off next 7 (9-11) sts, k to end. Cont on 22 (23-24) sts now rem on needle for left back and work 1 row. Cast off 3 (4-4) sts at beg of next row, 2 sts at same edge on next 2 alt rows and 1 st on next 2 alt rows. Work 5 rows straight then complete as for right front from ** to end. Rejoin correct colour to neck edge of right back sts, cast off 3 (4-4), p to end. Cast off 2 sts at same edge on next 2 alt rows and 1 st on next 2 alt rows; work 6 rows without shaping then complete as for right front from ** to end.

▦ **Sleeves** With 2¼mm needles and **B** cast on 38 (38-42) sts and work in rib as on front welt for 7 rows.

▦ *8th row* Rib 3 (4-3), [inc in next st, rib 7 (4-8)] 4 (6-4) times, inc in next st, rib 2 (3-2). 43 (45-47) sts. Change to 3mm needles and working in st st work striped patt as given for front but inc 1 st at both ends of every foll 6th row 7 (8-9) times. Cont on 57 (61-65) sts until 50 (54-58) rows have been worked in st st.

▦ **Top Shaping** Cast off 3 sts at beg of next 2 rows, 2 sts at beg of next 2 rows, 1 st at beg of next 4 (6-8) rows, 2 sts at beg of next 4 rows, 3 sts at beg of next 2 rows and 4 sts at beg of next 4 rows. Cast off rem 13 (15-17) sts.

▦ **Neck Borders** With right side facing and using 2¼mm needles and **B**, pick up and k 66 (70-74) sts along entire upper edge of front including the groups of sts cast off at end of neck shaping. Beg with 2nd row work in rib for 5 rows then cast off loosely in rib. Work similar border on upper edge of back picking up 74 (78-82) sts.

▦ **Finishing** Lap upper edge of back over front along armhole

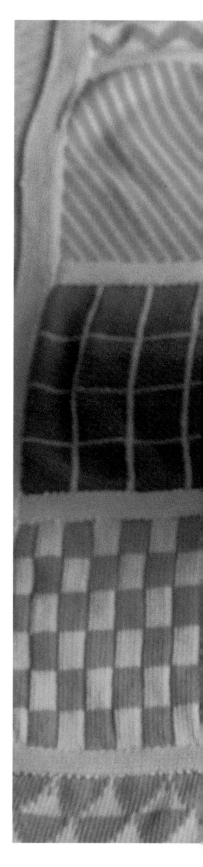

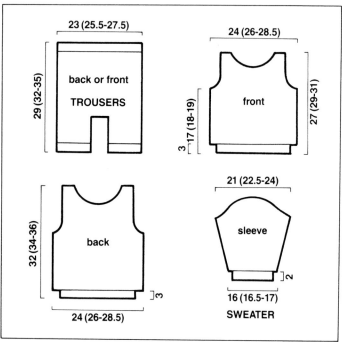

TROUSERS 23 (25.5-27.5)

back or front
TROUSERS
29 (32-35)

SWEATER front 24 (26-28.5)
3 · 17 (18-19) · 27 (29-31)

back
32 (34-36)
24 (26-28.5) · 3

sleeve
21 (22.5-24)
16 (16.5-17)
2

SWEATER

edges for a depth of 5cm (2in) and tack in place. Sew cast-off edges of sleeves to sides of armhole matching stripes and sewing through double thickness where back and front overlap. Remove tackings. Join side and sleeve seams matching stripes.

TROUSERS

▦ **Front** Beg at waist edge cast on 63 (69-75) sts using 2¾mm needles and **B**. Beg with a k row work in st st for 11 rows then k 1 row on wrong side for fold-line. Change to 3mm needles and beg with another k row cont in st st until work measures 20(22-24)cm, 7⅞(8⅝-9½)in, from beg, ending with a p row.
▦ *Next row* K 27 (30-33) and leave these sts on a spare needle, cast off 9, k to end. Cont on 27 (30-33) sts now rem on needle for one leg; cont until work measures 27(30-33)cm, 10⅝(11¾-13)in, from beg, ending with a k row. Change to 2¾mm needles and k 1 row for fold-line then work 7 rows in st st. Cast off loosely. Rejoin yarn to sts for other leg and complete in same way.

▦ **Back** Work exactly as for front.

▦ **Finishing** Join side seams then join inner leg and crotch seams making backstitch joins. Cut elastic to baby's waist measurement, overlap ends forming a ring and sew securely. Fold hem section at waist edge to inside enclosing elastic and hold edge in place with a row of herringbone st. Fold up hems on leg edges to inside and slip-st in place.

CHECKLIST

PATCHWORK BLANKET
Materials
*Sophie Desroches Coton Mat: 8 × 50g balls white (**A**) and 3 balls each peach (**B**), green (**C**) and orange (**D**). Pair each of needles size 2¾mm and 3mm.*

Size
Finished measurements 86cm× 96cm (33⅞in× 37¾in).

Stitches used
Single rib; st st; patts, as explained below.

Tension
Over st st and using 3mm needles, 27 sts and 36 rows to 10cm (4in). Work a sample on 32 sts. Some of the patts will give a slightly tighter tension and more sts are allowed for these. The finished rectangles should all measure approximately 16cm× 18cm (6¼in× 7⅛in).

INSTRUCTIONS

RECTANGLES

▦ The charts are worked 2, 3 or 4 times, using different colour combinations on various rectangles. The diagram shows the colours used and also the arrangement of rectangles. The arrow on each shows the direction of knitting. When they are joined some rectangles are placed sideways and some upside down to vary the effect.

▦ **Rectangle 1** With larger needles and **A** cast on 49 sts and working in st st work patt from Chart 1 using **D** and **A**.
▦ *1st row* K 6 **A**, * 1 **D**, 11 **A**; * rep from * to * ending 1 **D**, 6 **A**. Cont in patt as now arranged until work measures 18cm (7⅛in) from beg. Cast off.
▦ **Rectangle 2** With larger needles and **C** cast on 45 sts and working in st st work 2 rows **C**, [2 rows **A**, 8 rows **C**] 6 times, 2 rows **A**, 2 rows **C**. Cast off.
▦ **Rectangle 3** With larger

needles and **B** cast on 49 sts and working in st st work patt from Chart 2 using **B** and **A**.

▦ *1st row* K [1 **A**, 1 **B**] twice, 1 **A**, * 3 **B**, [1 **A**, 1 **B**] 4 times, 1 **A**; * rep from * to * twice more, 3 **B**, [1 **A**, 1 **B**] twice, 1 **A**. Cont in patt as now set until work measures 18cm (7⅛in) from beg. Cast off.

▦ **Rectangle 4** With larger needles and **A** cast on 49 sts and working in st st work patt from Chart 3 using **A** and **C**.

▦ *1st row* K 2 **A**, * 9 **C**, 3 **A**; * rep from * to * twice more, 9 **C**, 2 **A**. Cont in patt as now set until work measures 18cm (7⅛in) from beg. Cast off.

▦ **Rectangle 5** This is worked from side to side. With larger needles and **A** cast on 49 sts and working in st st work 2 rows **A** then [7 rows **D**, 5 rows **A**] 4 times, 7 rows **D**, 2 rows **A**. Cast off.

▦ **Rectangle 6** With larger

needles and **A** cast on 49 sts and working in st st work patt from Chart 4 using **A** and **B**.

▦ *1st row* * K 2 **B**, 2 **A**; rep from * to last st, 1 **B**.

▦ *2nd row* P 1 **B**, * 2 **A**, 2 **B**; rep from * to end.

▦ *3rd row* K 1 **A**, * 2 **B**, 2 **A**; rep from * to end. Cont in patt as now set until work measures 18cm (7⅛in) from beg. Cast off.

▦ **Rectangle 7** With larger needles and **D** cast on 49 sts and work as given for rectangle 3 but using **D** in place of **B**.

▦ **Rectangle 8** With larger needles and **A** cast on 49 sts and work as given for rectangle 1 but using **C** in place of **D**.

▦ **Rectangle 9** With larger needles and **B** cast on 45 sts and working in st st work 2 rows **B**, then [2 row **A**, 8 rows **B**] 6 times, 2 rows **A**, 2 rows **B**. Cast off.

▦ **Rectangle 10** With larger

needles and **A** cast on 50 sts and work in small check patt using **A** and **C** as foll:

▦ *1st row* K 1 **A**, * 6 **C**, 6 **A**; * rep from * to * 3 times more, 1 **C**.

▦ *2nd row* P 1 **A**, * 6 **A**, 6 **C**; * rep from * to * 3 times more, 1 **C**.

▦ *3rd to 10th rows* Rep 1st and 2nd rows 4 times more.

▦ *11th row* K 1 **C**, * 6 **A**, 6 **C**; * rep from * to * 3 times more, 1 **A**.

▦ *12th row* P 1 **C**, * 6 **C**, 6 **A**; * rep from * to * 3 times more, 1 **A**.

▦ *13th to 20th rows* Rep 11th and 12th rows 4 times more. Rep these 20 rows twice more or until work measures 18cm (7⅛in) from beg. Cast off.

▦ **Rectangle 11** This is worked in window-pane checks using **A** and **C**; only the horizontal stripes are knitted; the vertical stripes are worked on afterwards by the Swiss darning method as explained below. With larger

needles and **A** cast on 46 sts and working in st st work 2 rows **A**, then [14 rows **C**, 2 rows **A**] 4 times. Cast off. Thread a tapestry needle with a length of **A** and beg on 3rd row miss the first 10 sts from right-hand edge and on next 2 sts work a vertical stripe by the Swiss darning method as described on page 6. Work 2 more stripes in **A** missing 10 sts between them and leaving 10 sts at end.

▦ **Rectangle 12** This is worked from side to side. With larger needles and **A** cast on 49 sts and working in st st work 2 rows **A** then [7 rows **B**, 5 rows **A**] 4 times, 7 rows **B**, 2 rows **A**. Cast off.

▦ **Rectangle 13** Work as for rectangle 4 but using **D** in place of **C**.

▦ **Rectangle 14** With larger needles and **C** cast on 49 sts and working in st st work patt from

Chart 2 using **C** for the background with **A** for the triangles. Cont in patt until work measures 18cm (7⅛in) from beg. Cast off.

▧ **Rectangle 15** Work as for rectangle 6 but using **D** in place of **B**.

▧ **Rectangle 16** Work as for rectangle 10 but using **D** in place of **C**.

▧ **Rectangle 17** Work as for rectangle 4, using same colours.

▧ **Rectangle 18** Work as for rectangle 10 but using **B** instead of **C**.

▧ **Rectangle 19** With larger needles and **D** cast on 45 sts and working in st st work 2 rows **D**, then [2 rows **A**, 8 rows **D**] 6 times, 2 rows **A**, 2 rows **D**. Cast off.

▧ **Rectangle 20** Work as for rectangle 11 but using **B** in place of **C**.

▧ **Rectangle 21** Work as for rectangle 4 but using **B** in place of **C**.

▧ **Rectangle 22** Work as for rectangle 11 but using **D** in place of **C**.

▧ **Rectangle 23** This is worked from side to side. With larger needles and **A** cast on 49 sts and working in st st work 2 rows **A**, then [7 rows **C**, 5 rows **A**] 4 times, 7 rows **C**, 2 rows **A**. Cast off.

▧ **Rectangle 24** Work as for rectangle 1 but using **B** in place of **D**.

▧ **Rectangle 25** Work as for rectangle 6 but using **C** in place of **B**.

▧ **Strips** With larger needles and **A** cast on 6 sts and k 1 row.

▧ *2nd row* Slip 1 pw, p 5.

▧ *3rd row* Slip 1 kw, k 5. Rep last 2 rows until strip measures 80cm (31½in) long. Cast off. Work 3 more strips in same way. Now work 4 similar strips each 90cm (35½in) long.

▧ **Borders** With smaller needles and **A** cast on 13 sts for one side border.

▧ *1st row* K 2, [p 1, k 1] 5 times, k 1.

▧ *2nd row* [K 1, p 1] 6 times, k 1. Rep these 2 rows until border measures 96cm (37¾in) from beg. Cast off in rib. Work another border in same way. Work 2 borders for upper and lower edges each 80cm (31½in) long.

▧ **Finishing** Assemble the 25 rectangles as shown on the diagram, using a flat seam (see page 7). Press work on wrong side with warm iron and damp cloth. Now pin the narrow strips in place; with p side of strip to k side of main part pin the longer strips so that they cover the seams with the seam at centre of strip. There are almost bound to be minor differences in size between the finished patches. These can be evened out when you join them with the long strips if you first divide each strip equally into five, marking the divisions with pins. Pin the strips in position at these points and then carefully ease out any fullness when sewing. Slip-st the strips in place then pin and sew the shorter strips in place in same way. Sew shorter ribbed borders along upper and lower edges making backstitch joins then sew longer borders to side edges including ends of shorter borders.

Where one of the charts is used for working a rectangle the key to colours is shown above. Patterns used on the other rectangles are explained in the instructions. Arrows show the direction of knitting; take note of correct direction when sewing the rectangles together.

1 ↑ Chart 1 □ = White ✕ = Yellow	**2** ↑	**3** ↑ Chart 2 □ = Beige ✕ = White	**4** ↑ Chart 3 □ = White ✕ = Green	**5** ←
6 ↑ Chart 4 □ = White ✕ = Beige	**7** ↑ Chart 2 □ = Yellow ✕ = White	**8** ↑ Chart 1 □ = White ✕ = Green	**9** ↑	**10** ↑
11 ↑	**12** ←	**13** ↑ Chart 3 □ = White ✕ = Yellow	**14** ↓ Chart 2 □ = Green ✕ = White	**15** ↑ Chart 4 □ = White ✕ = Yellow
16 ↑	**17** ↑ Chart 3 □ = White ✕ = Green	**18** ↑	**19** ↑	**20** ↑
21 ↓ Chart 3 □ = White ✕ = Beige	**22** ↑	**23** ←	**24** ↑ Chart 1 □ = White ✕ = Beige	**25** ↑ Chart 4 □ = White ✕ = Green

Chart 1   12-row patt

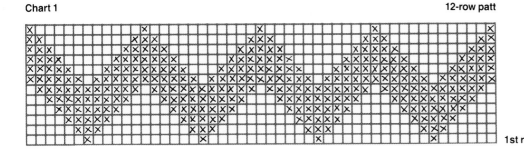

1st row

Chart 1

Use this chart for rectangles 1, 8 and 24. See diagram for colours. Chart shows full width; rep the 12-row patt until work is correct length.

Chart 2   20-row patt

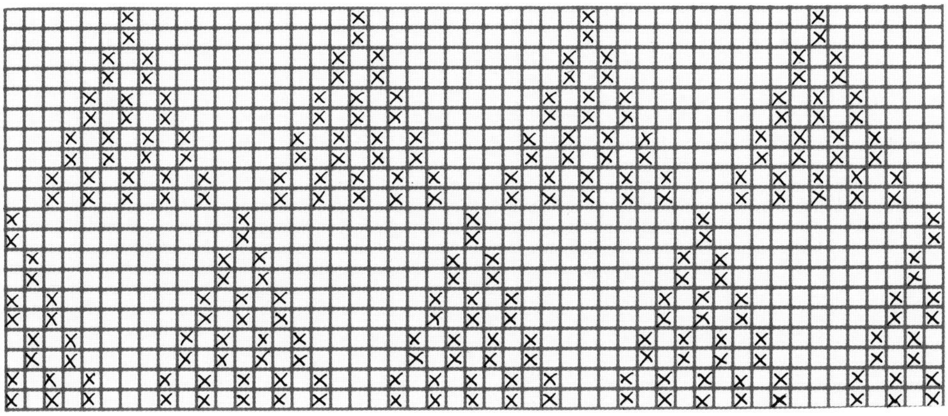

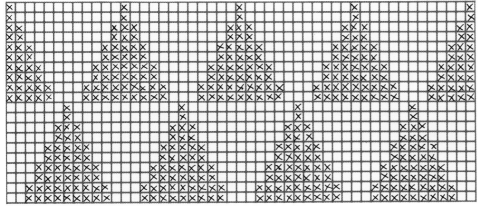

1st row

Chart 2

Use this chart for rectangles 3, 7 and 14. See diagram for colours. Chart shows full width; rep the 20-row patt until work is correct length.

Chart 3   20-row patt

1st row

Chart 3

Use this chart for rectangles 4, 13, 17 and 21. See diagram for colours. Chart shows full width; rep the 20-row patt until work is correct length.

Chart 4   8-row patt

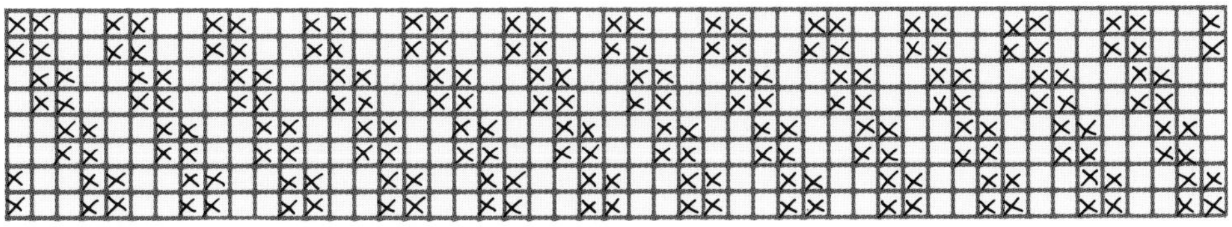

1st row

Chart 4

Use this chart for rectangles 6, 15 and 25. See diagram for colours. Chart shows full width; rep the 8-row patt until work is correct length.

FIRST BEST OUTFIT

This irresistably stylish outfit features the smart, multi-layered look – just the thing for your baby to wear when meeting an admiring host of grand-parents, aunts, uncles, friends and well-wishers. Knitted in a fine, soft yarn, it will keep baby warm without restricting his or her movements. Romper suit, buttoning down the back, bootees, socks and a pixie hat are all in garter stitch and rib. The finishing touch is a loose-fitting jacket in traditional Fair Isle patterns, adapted to make them easy to knit.

CHECKLIST

Materials

*For the complete set, Rowan 4-ply yarn: 6(7-7) × 25g balls pale grey (**A**); 2 balls rose pink (**B**), and one ball each green (**C**) and beige (**D**). Pair each of needles size 3mm and 3¼mm; 9 small buttons for rompers.*

Sizes

Rompers and jacket are in three sizes to fit ages 3 (6-9) months. Hat, socks and bootees are in two sizes to fit ages 3 to 6 (6 to 9) months. Actual measurements of rompers and jacket shown on diagrams.

Stitches used

Single rib; g st; st st; patt on the jacket is worked from charts as explained below. Some sections of the Fair Isle patt are embroidered on afterwards by the Swiss darning method and the small spot motifs on the rompers are also embroidered.

Tensions

Over g st using 3¼mm needles, 27 sts and 48 rows to 10cm (4in); work a sample on 32 sts. Over Fair Isle patt using 3¼mm needles, 31 sts and 32 rows to 10cm (4in); work a sample on 38 sts working from Chart 1 below.

INSTRUCTIONS

ROMPERS

☐ **Main Part** Beg at lower edge of right leg, cast on 60 (64-70) sts using smaller needles and **B**. Work in single rib working 2 rows **B** then change to **A** and cont in rib until work measures 7cm (2¾in) from beg. Change to larger needles and using **A** only work in g st counting 1st row as right side of work. Cont until work measures 15 (17-19)cm, 5⅞(6¾-7½)in, from beg, ending with a wrong-side row. ✲✲ Cut yarn and leave sts on a spare needle. Work left leg in same way as far as ✲✲ then join legs adding sts for gussets.

☐ *1st row* Cast on 10, k these sts and the sts of left leg, turn, cast on 20 sts; turn then, with right side facing, k the sts of right leg, turn and cast on 10 sts.

☐ *2nd row* K across 160 (168-180) sts.

☐ *3rd row* K 8, k 2 tog, k 60 (64-70), SKPO, k 16, k 2 tog, k 60 (64-70), SKPO, k 8.

☐ *4th row* K.

☐ *5th row* K 7, k 2 tog, k 60 (64-70), SKPO, k 14, k 2 tog, k 60 (64-70), SKPO, k 7. Cont working decs in these positions working 2 sts fewer at centre and 1 st at each end on 7th row then on every foll 4th row 4 times more.

☐ *24th row* K. Cast off 2 sts at beg of next 2 rows to make space for back borders to be worked afterwards. Cont on rem 128 (136-148) sts without shaping

until work measures 37(41-45)cm, 14½(16⅛-17¾)in, from beg, ending with a wrong-side row. Now divide for armholes.

☐ *Next row* K 31 (33-36), turn and cont on these sts for left back leaving rem sts on a spare needle. Cont in g st for 9(10-11)cm, 3½(4-4¼)in, ending at back opening edge.

☐ **Neck Shaping** Cast off 7 (8-9) sts at beg of next row and 4 sts at same edge on next 2 alt rows. Cast off rem 16 (17-19) sts for shoulder edge.

☐ **Front** With right side facing rejoin yarn to sts left unworked, k 66 (70-76) sts, turn and cont on these sts for front. Work 5(6-7)cm, 2(2⅜-2¾)in, without shaping, ending with a wrong-side row.

☐ **Neck Shaping** *1st row* K 27 (28-30) and leave these sts of left front on a spare needle, cast off next 12 (14-16) sts, k to end. Cont on 27 (28-30) sts now rem on needle for right front and k 1 row. ✲✲✲ Cast off 3 sts at beg of next row, 2 sts at same edge on next 2 alt rows and 1 st on next 4 alt rows. Cont on rem 16 (17-19) sts until work matches left back to shoulder. Cast off. Rejoin yarn to neck edge of left front sts and complete as for right front from ✲✲✲ to end.

☐ **Right Back** With right side facing rejoin yarn to rem 31 (33-36) sts left unworked at armhole opening, k to end. Complete as for left back reversing neck shaping.

☐ **Sleeves** With smaller needles and **B** cast on 36 (38-40) sts and work in single rib; work 2 rows in **B** then using **A** cont in rib until work measures 4cm (1½in) from beg.

☐ *Inc row* (wrong side) Rib 3 (1-4), [inc in next st, rib 5 (4-3)] 5 (7-8) times, inc in next st, rib 2 (1-3). 42 (46-49) sts. Change to 3¼mm needles and work in g st but inc 1 st at both ends of every foll 10th row 3 (4-4) times, then every foll 8th row 3 (3-4) times. Cont on 54 (60-65) sts until work measures 17(19-21)cm, 6¾(7½-8¼)in, from beg.

Cast off all sts.

☐ **Tie strip** With 3mm needles and **C** cast on 25 sts.

☐ *1st row* (right side) K 2, [p 1, k 1] 11 times, k 1.

☐ *2nd row* [K 1, p 1] 12 times, k 1. Rep these 2 rows 3 times more. Cast off in rib.

☐ **Back Borders** Beg above the 2 sts cast-off at end of gusset shaping, with right side of work facing and using smaller needles and **A**, pick up and k 82 (92-102) sts along left back edge. Work in single rib for 5 rows then cast off in rib. Work similar border on right back edge but after working 2 rows make buttonholes.

☐ *3rd row* Beg at lower edge, wrong side facing, rib 5 (7-9), cast off 2, [rib until there are 8 (9-10) sts on right needle after previous buttonhole, cast off 2] 7 times, rib to end. On foll row cast on 2 sts over each buttonhole. Rib 1 more row then cast off in rib.

☐ **Finishing and Neck Border** Join shoulder seams. With right side of work facing and using smaller needles and **A** pick up and k 22 (23-24) sts along left back neck edge including upper edge of back border, then 50 (52-54) sts around front neck edge and 22 (23-24) sts along right back edge including back border. 94 (98-102) sts. Work 2 rows in single rib.

☐ *3rd row* Beg at right back edge rib 2, cast off 2, rib to end. Change to **B** and cont in rib casting on 2 sts over buttonhole on next row then work 2 more rows. Cast off in rib.

☐ Before sewing rem seams work the motifs all over g st sections; thread a tapestry needle with 2 strands of **B** and sew twice over 2 sts and 2 rows, cut ends and tie close to work. Space knots approximately 9 sts and 18 rows apart in alternating positions as shown. Join sleeve seams and sew cast-off edge into armholes. Join inner leg seams and sew across cast-on edges of gussets. At back join outer edges of gussets below back borders. Sew centre of tie strip to front just below neck border stitching tightly across centre to simulate a bow. Sew on buttons to correspond with buttonholes and slip-st lower edges of borders in place lapping right border over left.

JACKET

▦ **Main Part** This is worked in one piece up to armhole openings. With smaller needles and **B** cast on 141 (153-165) sts and work in rib.

▦ *1st row* (right side) P 1, * k 1, p 1; rep from * to end.

▦ *2nd row* K 1, * p 1, k 1; rep from * to end. K 1 row in **B**.

▦ *4th row* K 12 (14-16), [inc in next st, k 28 (30-32)] 4 times, inc in next st, k 12 (14-16). 146 (158-170) sts. Change to larger needles and working in st st work patt from Chart 1.

▦ *1st row* K 2 **B**, * 2 **A**, 2 **B**; rep from * to end. Cont working from chart for a further 5 (9-13) rows. Now work from Chart 2; note that the sts shown in **C** are embroidered on afterwards and they should be worked in **A** on the 10 rows of chart as foll:

▦ *1st row* K 2 **A**, * 2 **B**, 2 **A**; rep from * to end. Work 8 more rows with colours as set.

▦ *10th row* * P 3 **A**, 1 **B**; rep from * to last 2 sts, 2 **A**. Change to smaller needles and work in g st working 2 rows **C**, 2 rows **A**, 2 rows **B** but on last of these rows, for 1st size inc 1 st at centre (for 3rd size dec 1 st at centre). Change back to larger needles and cont on 147 (158-169) sts, working patt from Chart 3; note that the sts shown in **D** and the single st in **C** at centre of each motif are all embroidered on afterwards so these should be worked in **B**. When working more than 5 sts in **A** or **B** twist the other colour around the yarn in use once at centre of the group of sts; do not weave in as this distorts the tension.

▦ *1st row* K 4 **B**, * 7 **A**, 4 **B**; rep from * to end.

▦ *2nd row* P 5 **B**, * 5 **A**, 6 **B**; rep from * to last 10 sts, 5 **A**, 5 **B**. Cont as now set until chart is completed. Cut yarn and slip all

sts onto a smaller needle so that right side will be facing for next row. Using **B** k 1 row but for 1st size dec 1 st at centre (for 3rd size inc 1 st at centre). 146 (158-170) sts. Cont in g st and work 1 more row in **B** then 2 rows **A** and 2 rows **C**. Change back to larger needles and working in st st work patt from Chart 1, *at same time* dividing for armhole openings.

▫ *1st row* K [2 **B**, 2 **A**] 9 (10-11) times, 2 (1-0) **B**, turn and cont on these sts for right front, leaving rem sts on a spare needle. Cont on these 38 (41-44) sts keeping patt correct until work measures 6(7-8)cm, 2⅜(2¾-3⅛)in, from beg of this patt section, ending at front edge after a p row.

▫ **Neck Shaping** Cast off 10 (11-12) sts at beg of next row, 4 sts at same edge on next alt row, 2 sts on next 2 alt rows and 1 st on next 3 alt rows. Cont on rem 17 (19-21) sts until work measures 11(12-13)cm, 4¼(4¾-5⅛)in, from beg of this patt section. Cast off all sts.

▫ **Back** With right side facing and using larger needles, rejoin yarn to sts unworked and cont in patt; k 0 (1-2) **B**, [2 **A**, 2 **B**] 17 (18-19) times, 2 **A**, 0 (1-2) **B**, turn and cont on these 70 (76-82) sts for back; keep patt correct and cont without shaping until work matches right front to shoulder edge.
Cast off all sts.

▫ **Left Front** With right side facing and using larger needles, rejoin yarn to rem 38 (41-44) sts, k 2 (1-0) **B**, [2 **A**, 2**B**] 9 (10-11) times. Cont in patt and complete as for right front reversing neck shaping.

▫ **Sleeves** With smaller needles and **B** cast on 57 (61-65) sts and work 2 rows in rib as on main part. K 1 row in **B**.

▫ *4th row* K 7 (9-11), [inc in next st, k 13] 3 times, inc in next st, k 7 (9-11). 61 (65-69) sts. Change to larger needles and working in st st work patt from Chart 4.

▫ *1st row* K 1 **A**, * 3 **B**, 1 **A**; rep from * to end.

▫ *2nd row* P 2 **A**, * 1 **B**, 3 **A**; rep from * ending 1 **B**, 2 **A**. Cont in

patt as now set but inc 1 st at both ends of every foll 8th row twice then every foll 6th row 2 (3-4) times working extra sts into patt. Cont on 69 (75-81) sts until work measures 13(15-17)cm, 5⅛(5⅞-6¾)in, from beg, ending with a p row. Change to smaller needles and working in g st work 2 rows **B**, 2 rows **A**, 2 rows **C**. Cast off all sts.

▫ **Finishing and Borders** First complete the panels of patt worked from Charts 2 and 3 by covering the sts shown by these symbols in the correct colour using the Swiss darning method described on page 6. To neaten front edges, with right side facing and using smaller needles and **B**, pick up and k 51 (57-63) sts along front edge of right front. P 1 row then cast off. Work similar edging on left front. Fold edgings inside and slip-st in place on wrong side.

▫ Sew shoulder edges of fronts to a corresponding width on top edge of back leaving centre 36 (38-40) sts of back free for neckline. With right side of work facing and using smaller needles and **B**, pick up and k 27 (28-29) sts along right front neck edge, 35 (37-39) sts across back neck and 27 (28-29) sts along left front neck. 89 (93-97) sts. K 1 row on wrong side then rep 1st and 2nd rows of rib border twice. Cast off in rib. Join sleeve seams. Sew cast-off edge of sleeves to sides of armhole openings.

SOCKS (both alike)

▫ Beg at upper edge cast on 52 (60) sts using smaller needles and **C**. Work in single rib for 11(12)cm, 4¼(4¾)in. Change to **B** and still using smaller needles work in g st counting 1st row as right side row. Work 10 rows in **B** then change to **D** and begin shaping.

▫ *11th row* K 2 tog, * k 23 (27), k 2 tog; rep from * once. Work 3 rows on rem 49 (57) sts.

▫ *15th row* K 2 tog, k 21 (25), k 2 tog, k 22 (26), k 2 tog. Work 1 (3) rows in **D** then change to **C** and work 2 (0) rows.

▫ *19th row* K 2 tog, * k 20 (24), k 2 tog; rep from * once. Cont to dec at each end of row and at centre, on every foll 4th row 5 (6) times more, and at same time cont stripes: work 7 (9) more rows in **C**, then 2 rows in **B**, 6 rows in **A** and 6 (8) rows in **D**. Decs have been completed, 28 (33) sts rem. Cont with **D** and work in st st; work 7(8)cm, 2¾(3⅛)in, ending with a p row, then shape toe.

▫ *1st row* [K 2 tog] 14 (16) times, k 0 (1). P 1 row.

▫ *3rd row* [K 2 tog] 7 (8) times, k 0 (1). Cut yarn, pass it through rem sts, draw up tightly and sew securely then join seam along foot and back of leg, matching stripes.

BOOTEES (both alike)

▫ Beg at upper edge cast on 40 (48) sts using smaller needles and **B**; work in g st for 23 rows then make holes for cord.

▫ *24th row* K 1, [k 2 tog, yfd, k 2] 9 (11) times, k 2 tog, yfd, k 1. Work 6 (8) more rows in g st then shape heel.

▫ *1st row* K 8 (10), turn and cont on these sts for one side of heel leaving rem sts on a spare needle. Cont in g st and dec 1 st at outer edge on next row and next 3 (4) alt rows. Cast off rem 4 (5) sts. Return to sts left unworked, slip next 24 (28) sts of instep onto a holder, rejoin yarn to rem 8 (10) sts, k to end. Complete as for first side of heel reversing shapings.

▫ With right side facing pick up and k 8 (10) sts along straight side edge of first heel section, k sts of instep then pick up and k 8 (10) sts along straight side of second heel section. Work 3 (7) rows on these 40 (48) sts then shape foot.

▫ *1st row* K 5 (7), SKPO, k 2,

KEY
▫ pale grey
▫ rose pink
▫ green
▫ beige

Charts 1, 2 and 3 are used for the main part of the jacket (in order 1, 2, 3 and then 1 again), and chart 4 is used for the sleeves only.

k 2 tog, k 18 (22), SKPO, k 2, k 2 tog, k 5 (7). Work 5 rows straight.

▫ *7th row* K 4 (6), SKPO, k 2, k 2 tog, k 16 (20), SKPO, k 2, k 2 tog, k 4 (6). Cont to work 4 decs in these positions, working 2 sts fewer at centre and 1 st at sides, on every foll 6th row 3 (4) times more. K 1 row on rem 20 (24) sts.

▫ *Next row* [K 2 tog] 10 (12) times. K 1 row.

▫ *Next row* [K 2 tog] 5 (6) times. Cut yarn, thread end through rem sts, draw up tightly and sew securely then join seam along foot and back of leg. Make a length of twisted cord and thread through holes at ankle to tie at front.

HAT

▫ With smaller needles and **B** cast on 90 (98) sts and work in single rib; work 2 rows in **B** then change to **A** and cont in rib until work measures 13(14)cm, 5⅛(5½)in, from beg. Still using smaller needles work in g st counting 1st row as right side. Work 4 rows then begin shaping.

▫ *5th row* K 2 tog, * k 42 (46), k 2 tog; rep from * once. Work 3 rows on rem 87 (95) sts.

▫ *9th row* K 2 tog, k 40 (44), k 2 tog, k 41 (45), k 2 tog. Work 3 rows on rem 84 (92) sts.

▫ *13th row* K 2 tog, * k 39 (43), k 2 tog; rep from * once. Cont to dec at each end and at centre of row on every foll 4th row 21 (22) times more. K 1 row on rem 18 (23) sts.

▫ *Next row* [K 2 tog] 9 (11) times, k 0 (1). Cut yarn, pass it through rem sts, draw up tightly and sew securely then sew back seam of hat reversing it on brim. Make a large pom-pon using **B**, **C** and **D**; sew it to point.

. Chart no 1

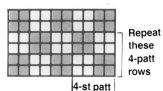

Repeat these 4-patt rows

4-st patt

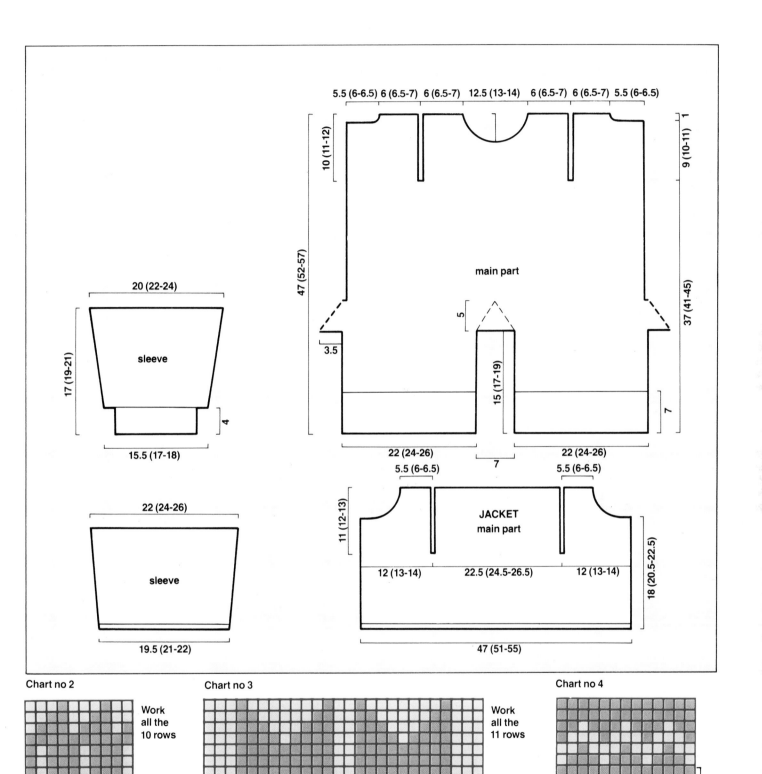

5.5 (6-6.5) 6 (6.5-7) 6 (6.5-7) 12.5 (13-14) 6 (6.5-7) 6 (6.5-7) 5.5 (6-6.5)

10 (11-12)

9 (10-11) 1

47 (52-57)

main part

37 (41-45)

5

3.5

15 (17-19)

7

22 (24-26)

7

22 (24-26)

20 (22-24)

sleeve

17 (19-21)

4

15.5 (17-18)

22 (24-26)

sleeve

19.5 (21-22)

5.5 (6-6.5)

5.5 (6-6.5)

11 (12-13)

JACKET
main part

18 (20.5-22.5)

12 (13-14)   22.5 (24.5-26.5)   12 (13-14)

47 (51-55)

Chart no 2

Work
all the
10 rows

|4-st patt|

*Sts shown by the symbol for **C**
should be worked in **A** and
embroidered afterwards.*

Chart no 3

Work
all the
11 rows

11-st patt

*Sts shown by the symbols for **C** and **D** should be worked in **B**
and embroidered afterwards.*

Chart no 4

4-st patt

Repeat these 6-patt rows

STYLISH AND PRACTICAL

Playing it cool and remaining seated when his girl friend comes to visit him – perhaps this young man's fashion sense is in advance of his manners? This smart yet practical outfit has great style and could prove particularly useful for a chubby youngster who tends to find cloth trousers just too tight across his middle. The cardigan is knitted in stocking stitch and the amusing patches in bright colours are added afterwards. The trousers are knitted in double stranded yarn to give extra strength and firmness.

CHECKLIST

Materials
Brushed 4-ply yarn: 3 (4-4) × 50g balls grey for cardigan and 4 (5-6) balls grey for trousers. For the contrast patches on the cardigan, 4-ply yarn: one ball or part-ball yellow, red and green. Pair each of needles sizes 2¾mm, 3mm, 3¾mm and 4mm; a cable needle; 5 buttons in different colours for the cardigan; 2 buttons for the trousers.

Sizes
Three sizes to fit ages 12 months (18 months–2 years). Actual measurements shown on diagram.

Stitches used
Single rib; st st; double rib; rib and cable patt, *worked on trousers, is explained in the instructions. Cable 4 front = slip next 2 sts on cable needle, leave at front, k 2, then k 2 from cable needle.*

Tension
Over st st using 3mm needles and yarn single, 28 sts and 36 rows to 10cm (4in); work a sample on 34 sts. Over rib and cable patt using 4mm needles and yarn double, 24 sts and 27 rows to 10cm (4in); work a sample on 32 sts arranging patt on 1st row thus, [p 2, k 2] 4 times, p 2, k 4 for a cable, [p 2, k 2] 4 times, p 2. Flatten sample out when measuring.

INSTRUCTIONS

CARDIGAN

▦ **Back** With 2¾mm needles cast on 81 (87-93) sts and work in rib.

▦ *1st row* (right side) P 1, * k 1, p 1; rep from * to end.

▦ *2nd row* K 1, * p 1, k 1; rep from * to end. Rep these 2 rows until work measures 3.5cm (1⅜in) from beg, ending with a 2nd rib row. Change to 3mm needles and beg with a k row work in st st. Cont until work measures 15(17-19)cm, 5⅞(6¾-7½)in, from beg, ending with a p row.

▦ **Armhole Shaping** Cast off 3 sts at beg of next 2 rows, 2 sts at beg of next 2 rows and 1 st at beg of next 10 rows. Cont on rem 61 (67-73) sts until work measures 26(29-32)cm, 10¼(11⅜-12⅝)in, from beg, ending with a p row.

▦ **Shoulder and Neck Shaping** Cast off 6 (6-7) sts at beg of next 2 rows.

▦ *3rd row* Cast off 6 (6-7), k until there are 11 (13-13) sts on right needle, leave these for right back, cast off next 15 (17-19) sts, k to end.

▦ Cont on 17 (19-20) sts now rem at end of needle for left back. Cast off 6 (6-7) sts at beg of next row and 5 sts at neck edge on foll row. Cast off rem 6 (8-8) sts to complete shoulder slope. Rejoin yarn to neck edge of right back sts, cast off 5, p to end. Cast off rem 6 (8-8) sts.

▦ **Left Front** With 2¾mm needles cast on 39 (43-45) sts and work in rib as on back welt for same number of rows but for 1st and 3rd sizes inc 1 st in centre of last row. 40 (43-46) sts. Change to 3mm needles and work in st st; cont until work measures 15(17-19)cm, 5⅞(6¾-7½)in, from beg, ending with a p row.

▦ **Armhole and Front Shaping**
1st row Cast off 3 to begin armhole, k to last 2 sts, k 2 tog to begin front shaping. Cast off at armhole edge on alt rows 2 sts once and 1 st 5 times; *at same time*, dec 1 st at front edge on every row 11 (12-13) times more. When all shapings are completed cont on rem 18 (20-22) sts until work matches back to beg of shoulder, ending at armhole edge.

▦ **Shoulder Shaping** Cast off 6 (6-7) sts at beg of next row and next alt row, work 1 row then cast off rem 6 (8-8) sts.

▦ **Right Front** Work as for left front reversing all shapings.

▦ **Sleeves** With 2¾mm needles cast on 43 (45-49) sts and work in rib as on back welt for 3cm (1⅛in) ending with a 2nd rib row. Change to 3mm needles and work in st st but inc 1 st at both ends of every foll 6th row 8 (8-9) times, then every foll 4th row 0 (2-2) times. Cont on 59 (65-71) sts until work measures 18(20-22)cm, 7⅛(7⅞-8⅝)in, from beg.

▦ **Top Shaping** Cast off 3 sts at beg of next 2 rows, 2 sts at beg of next 2 rows, 1 st at beg of next 18 (16-14) rows, 2 sts at beg of next 4 (6-8) rows and 3 (4-5) sts at beg of next 2 rows. Cast off rem 17 (19-21) sts.

▦ **Front border** With 3mm needles cast on 6 sts.

▦ *1st row* (right side) K.

▦ *2nd row* K 1, p 4, k 1.

▦ *3rd row* K 1, cable 4 front, k 1.

▦ *4th row* As 2nd. These 4 rows form one patt. Cont in patt for 3 (3-1) rows then begin making buttonholes.

▦ *Next row* (wrong side) K 1, p 2, tog, yrn, p 2, k 1. ** Work 9 (11-13) rows in patt then make

another buttonhole on next row; rep from ** 3 times more. Cont in patt until border when slightly stretched fits along both front edges and across back neck. Leave sts on a safety pin without cutting yarn so that length can be adjusted.

▦ **Patches** Before sewing garment work the patches using the Swiss darning method described on page 6. Work the triangles, squares and circles in the positions indicated on diagrams using the colours shown.

▦ **Finishing** Join shoulder seams, sew in sleeves then join side and sleeve seams. Pin front border in place with buttonholes to left front for a boy or right front for a girl, stretching border slightly around neck edges so that it sits well. Replace sts on needle, adjust length if necessary so that it reaches to lower edge of right or left front then cast off. Sew border in place as pinned. Sew on buttons to correspond with buttonholes.

TROUSERS

▦ These are worked entirely in double-stranded yarn; take one ball and wind it into 2 equal balls then rewind these tog to form a double stranded ball which is easier to use.

▦ **Front** Beg at waist edge cast on 83 (87-91) sts using 3¾mm needles. Work in rib as given for cardigan and then after working 4 rows make buttonholes as foll:

▦ *5th row* Rib 21 (22-23), cast off 2, rib until there are 37 (39-41) sts on right needle after previous buttonhole, cast off 2, rib to end.

▦ *6th row* Rib 21 (22-23), turn, cast on 2, turn, rib 37 (39-41), turn, cast on 2, turn, rib 21 (22-23). Work 4 more rows in rib and inc 1 st in centre of last row. 84 (88-92) sts. Change to 4mm needles and work in rib and cable patt.

▦ *1st row* (right side) P 2 (0-2), [k 2, p 2] 4 (5-5) times, * k 4 for a cable, [p 2, k 2] 4 times, p 2; * rep

from * to * once, k 4 for a cable, [p 2, k 2] 4 (5-5) times, p 2 (0-2).

□ *2nd row* K 2 (0-2), [p 2, k 2] 4 (5-5) times, * p 4, [k 2, p 2] 4 times, k 2; * rep from * to * once, p 4, [k 2, p 2] 4 (5-5) times, k 2 (0-2).

□ *3rd row* Rib 18 (20-22) as on 1st row, * cable 4 front, rib 18; * rep from * to * once, cable 4 front, rib 18 (20-22).

□ *4th row* As 2nd. These 4 rows form one patt. Cont in patt until work measures 19(20-21)cm, 7½(7⅞-8¼)in, from beg, ending with a wrong-side row. Now divide for legs.

□ *Next row* Patt 40 (42-44), k

next 2 sts, turn and cont on these 42 (44-46) sts for one leg leaving rem sts on a spare needle. **
Work only one cable and keep rem sts in rib; dec 1 st at both ends of every foll 8th row 0 (3-6) times, then every foll 6th row 5 (3-0) times, then every foll 4th row 1 (0-0) times. Cont on rem 30 (32-34) sts until work measures 34(38-42)cm, 13⅜(15-16½)in, from beg, ending with a wrong-side row and working 1 dec at centre of last row. 29 (31-33) sts.

□ Change to 3¾mm needles and work in single rib; work 4 rows straight, dec 1 st at both ends of next row then work 5

more rows in rib.

□ Cast off loosely ribwise. Rejoin yarn with right side facing to sts left unworked, k 2, patt to end. Complete as for first leg from ** to end.

□ **Back** Work as for left leg omitting buttonholes.

□ **Shoulder Straps** Make 2 alike. With 3¾mm needles cast on 8 sts.

□ *1st row* (right side) K 3, p 2, k 3.

□ *2nd row* K 1, p 2, k 2, p 2, k 1. Rep these 2 rows until strap measures 46(50-54)cm, 18(19¾-21¼)in, from beg. Cast off.

□ **Instep Straps** Make 2 alike. With 3¾mm needles cast on 4 sts.

□ *1st row* K 2, p 1, k 1. Rep this row until strap measures 12(14-16)cm, 4¾(5½-6¼)in, from beg. Cast off.

□ **Finishing** Join side seams and inner leg seams. Sew shoulder straps to back waistband and sew a button to other end of each strap. Sew instep straps to each side of the legs so that they will pass easily underneath the foot when worn, like ski pants.

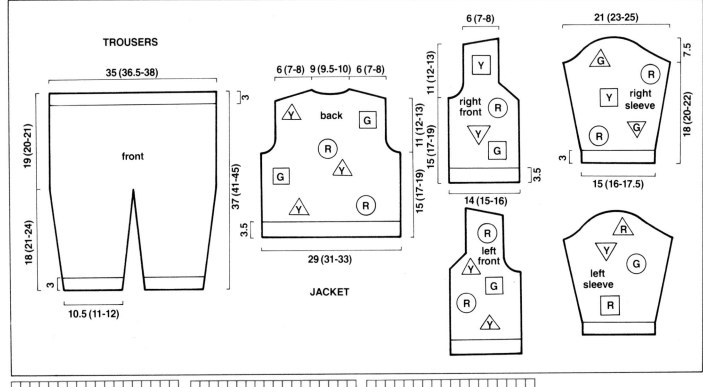

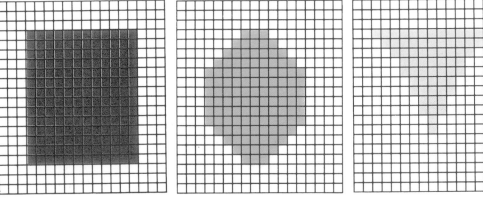

For the patches work shapes as shown on diagram placing them on back, fronts and sleeves as shown above; note that some of the triangles have the apex at the top and some at the bottom. Use the Swiss darning method on page 6. The exact placing of the motifs is not crucial, but you may find it easier to achieve a balanced arrangement if you first cut out paper circles, squares and triangles and pin them in place on the knitting.

COLOURFUL CAROLINE

Here is an outfit designed to turn baby tears to chuckles of delighted laughter. This adorable twinset is knitted and decorated in a colour combination modelled on glorious chintz fabric and evocative of a bouquet of summer flowers. The cardigan is embroidered all over with dots of colour, which are echoed in the varied stripes of the sweater. The irresistably pretty bootees are also decorated with coloured spots, but the cardigan would make a delightful gift on its own.

CHECKLIST

Materials
*Pingouin Fine + : 3 (4) × 50g balls cream (**A**), one ball or part-ball each pale green (**B**), yellow (**C**), orange (**D**), dark lavender (**E**), raspberry red (**F**), gold (**G**), and red (**H**).*
Also a small amount of yarn in a tan shade for some of the spots on the cardigan.
Pair each of needles size 2¾mm and 3¼mm.
5 buttons for cardigan, 3 buttons for sweater and 2 buttons for bootees.

Sizes
Cardigan and sweater, two sizes, to fit ages 6 to 9 (12 to 18) months. Actual measurements shown on diagrams. Bootees in one size to fit a baby up to 9 months.

Stitches used
Single rib; st st; g st; k loop = pick up loop lying between needles and k it through the back. The spots are worked on afterwards.

Tension
Over st st using 3¼mm needles, 28 sts and 36 rows to 10cm (4in). Work a sample on 34 sts.

INSTRUCTIONS

CARDIGAN

⊞ **Back** With smaller needles and **A** cast on 69 (75) sts and work in rib.
⊞ *1st row* (right side) P 1, * k 1, p 1; rep from * to end.
⊞ *2nd row* K 1, * p 1, k 1; rep from * to end. Rep these 2 rows 3 times more then 1st row again.
⊞ *10th row* Rib 13 (15), [inc in next st, rib 13 (14)] 4 times. 73 (79) sts. Change to larger needles and beg with a k row work in st st. Cont until work measures 15(17)cm, 5⅞(6¾)in, from beg, ending with a p row.
⊞ **Armhole Shaping** Cast off 2 sts at beg of next 2 rows and 1 st

at beg of next 6 rows. Cont on rem 63 (69) sts until work measures 26.5(29.5)cm, 10½(11⅝)in, from beg, ending with a p row.
⊞ **Shoulder and Neck Shaping** *1st row* Cast off 8 (9), k until there are 14 (15) sts on right needle, leave these for right back, cast off 19 (21) sts, k to end. Cont on 22 (24) sts now rem at end of needle for left back. Cast off 8 (9) sts at beg of next row and 5 sts at neck edge on foll row. Cast off rem 9 (10) sts to complete shoulder slope. Rejoin yarn to neck edge of right back sts, cast off 5, p to end. Cast off rem 9 (10) sts.

⊞ **Left front** With smaller

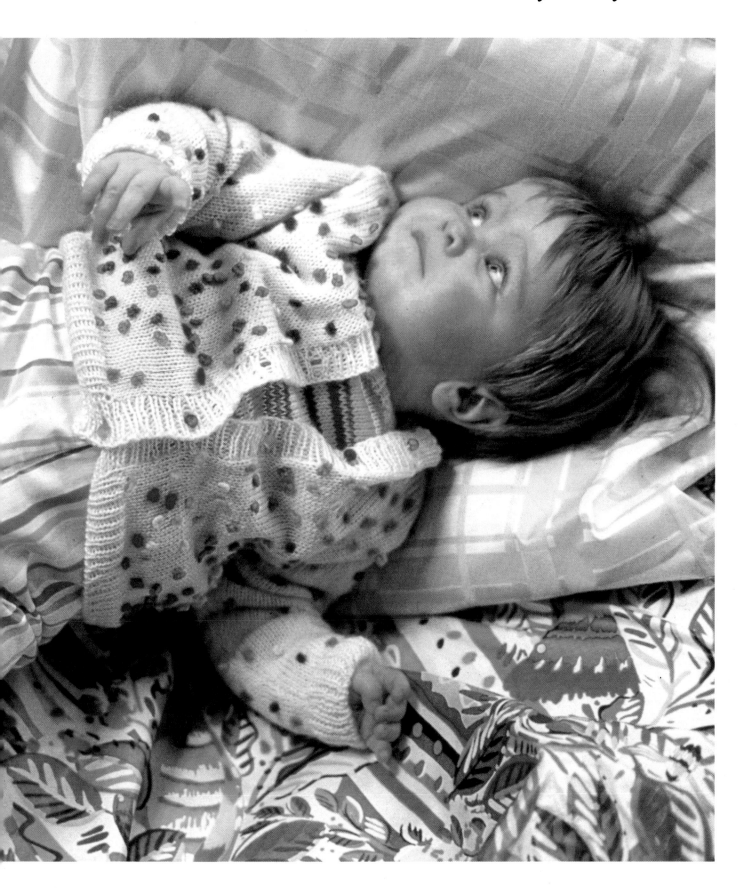

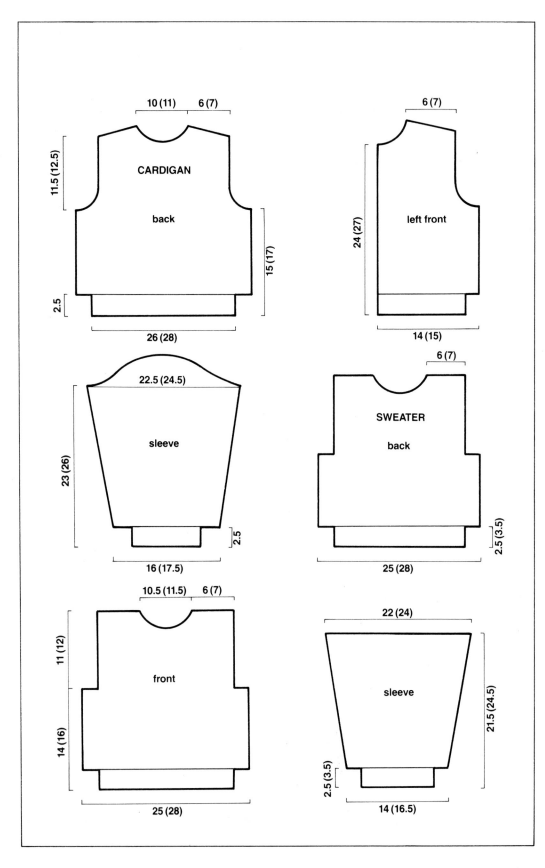

10 (11)   6 (7)

11.5 (12.5)

CARDIGAN

back

15 (17)

2.5

26 (28)

6 (7)

24 (27)

left front

14 (15)

22.5 (24.5)

sleeve

23 (26)

2.5

16 (17.5)

6 (7)

SWEATER

back

2.5 (3.5)

25 (28)

10.5 (11.5)   6 (7)

11 (12)

front

14 (16)

25 (28)

22 (24)

sleeve

21.5 (24.5)

2.5 (3.5)

14 (16.5)

needles and **A** cast on 37 (39) sts and work in rib as for back welt for 9 rows then rib 1 more row working 2 (3) incs evenly spaced. 39 (42) sts. Change to larger needles and work in st st until work matches back to beg of armhole ending with a p row.

▦ **Armhole Shaping** Cast off 2 sts at beg of next row and next alt row and 1 st at same edge on next 2 alt rows. Cont on rem 33 (36) sts until work measures 24(27)cm, 9½(10⅝)in, from beg, ending at front edge.

▦ **Neck and Shoulder Shaping** Cast off 7 (8) sts at beg of next row, 3 sts at same edge on next alt row, 2 sts on next 2 alt rows and 1 st on next alt row. Cast off 8 (9) sts for shoulder at beg of next row and dec 1 st at neck edge on foll row. Cast off rem 9 (10) sts.

▦ **Right Front** Work as for left front reversing all shapings.

▦ **Sleeves** With smaller needles and **A** cast on 39 (43) sts and work in rib for 9 rows.
▦ *Inc row* Rib 2 (4), [inc in next st, rib 6] 5 times, inc in next st, rib 1 (3). 45 (49) sts. Change to larger needles and work in st st but inc 1 st at both ends of every foll 8th row 6 times, then every foll 6th row 3 (4) times. Cont on 63 (69) sts until work measures 23(26)cm, 9(10¼)in, from beg.

▦ **Top Shaping** Cast off 3 sts at beg of next 2 rows, 2 sts at beg of next 4 rows, 1 st at beg of next 6 rows, 2 sts at beg of next 8 (10) rows and 4 sts at beg of next 2 rows. Cast off rem 19 (21) sts.

▦ **Front Borders** With right side of work facing and using smaller needles and **A**, pick up and k 71 (79) sts along front edge of left front. Work in rib beg with 2nd row; if for a girl work 9 rows in rib then cast off in rib. If for a boy work 3 rows then make buttonholes.
▦ *Next row* Beg at neck edge rib 13 (15), * cast off 2, [rib until there are 15 (17) sts on right needle after previous buttonhole, cast off 2] 3 times, * rib to end. On foll row cast on 2 sts over each

buttonhole. Work 4 more rows in rib then cast off in rib. Pick up same number of sts on right front and work in rib. If for a boy work 9 rows in rib then cast off in rib. If for a girl work 3 rows in rib then make buttonholes.

▦ *Next row* Beg at lower edge rib 5, rep from * to * in same row of left front border, rib to end. On foll row cast on 2 sts over each buttonhole, work 4 more rows in rib then cast off in rib.

▦ Finishing and Neck Border

Join shoulder seams. With right side of work facing and using smaller needles and **A**, pick up and k 9 sts across top of right front border, 19 (20) sts along right front neck edge, 33 (35) sts across back neck, 19 (20) sts along left front neck edge and 9 sts across top of left front border. 89 (93) sts.

▦ Beg with 2nd row, work in rib and after working 1 row make another buttonhole above previous ones on next 2 rows. Work 4 more rows in rib then cast off in rib.

▦ Before sewing rem seams embroider spots in a random arrangement using the other colours; to form a spot thread a tapestry needle with a double length of yarn, bring needle through to right side, insert needle under 2 sts of knitting in same place, wind yarn 5 times around point of needle then, holding the strands in place with left thumb, draw the needle through. Tighten knot and darn in end securely on wrong side.

▦ When spots are completed sew in sleeves then join side and sleeve seams. Sew on buttons to correspond with buttonholes.

SWEATER

▦ **Stripe sequence for back and front** Working in st st, work 1 row **B**, 1 row **A**, 2 rows **B**, 2 rows **G**, 1 row **F**, 2 rows **B**, 1 row **A**, 3 rows **E**, 1 row **A**, 2 rows **C**, 3 rows **A**, 5 (6) rows **G**, 1 row **A**, 1 row **H**, 1 row **A**, 2 rows **B**, 1 row **A**, 5 (6) rows **D**, [1 row **A**, 1 row **B**] twice, 1 row **C**, 1 row **E**, 4 (5) rows **C**, 4

(5) rows **A**, * 2 rows **E**, 3 (4) rows **A**, 3 rows **H**, 1 row **B**, 1 row **E**, 5 (6) rows **B**, 2 rows **A**, 2 (3) rows **G**, 4 (5) rows **A**, * 1 row **B**, 1 row **A**, 2 rows **B**, 2 rows **G**, 1 row **F**, 3 rows **B**.

▦ These 82 (90) rows form complete patt for back and front.

▦ **Stripe sequence for sleeves** Working in st st, work from * to * as given for back and front, then work the first 45 (49) rows of the sequence for back and front; these 68 (76) rows complete patt for sleeves.

▦ **Back** With smaller needles and **A** cast on 65 (71) sts and work in rib as on cardigan for 9 (13) rows.

▦ *Inc row* Rib 6 (9), [inc in next st, rib 12] 4 times, inc in next st, rib 6 (9). 70 (76) sts. Change to larger needles and working in st st beg with a k row work stripe sequence as above. Cont until 42 (46) rows have been worked thus ending with 1 (3) rows of stripes in **C**.

▦ **Armhole Shaping** Cast off 3 sts at beg of next 2 rows then cont on rem 64 (70) sts until 78 (86) rows have been worked in patt.

▦ **Neck Shaping** *Next row* With **F**, k 20 (22) and leave these sts of right back on needle, cast off next 24 (26) sts, k to end. Cont on 20 (22) sts now rem at end of needle for left back and using B, dec 1 st at neck edge on next 3 rows. 17 (19) sts. Change to smaller needles and work shoulder border using **B**.

▦ *Inc row* * [P 1, k 1] twice, inc in next st; rep from * once, then [p 1, k 1] 3 (4) times, p 1. Beg with 2nd row cont in rib on these 19 (21) sts and work 5 more rows then cast off in rib. With wrong side facing and using larger needles, rejoin B to sts of right back; dec 1 st at neck edge on next 3 rows then cast off rem 17 (19) sts.

▦ **Front** Work as for back until 68 (76) rows have been worked thus ending with 2 (3) rows in **G**.

▦ **Neck Shaping** *Next row* With **A**, k 26 (28) and leave these sts of left front on a spare needle, cast off next 12 (14) sts, k to end. Cont

on 26 (28) sts now rem on needle for right front keeping patt correct and work 1 row without shaping. ** Cast off 3 sts at beg of next row, 2 sts at same edge on next 2 alt rows and 1 st on next 2 alt rows. ** Work 3 rows in **B** to complete patt. Cast off rem 17 (19) sts. Rejoin **A** to neck edge of left front sts and cont as for right front from ** to **. Change to smaller needles and **B**. Rep the inc row given on left back shoulder then cont in rib; work 1 row then make buttonholes.

▦ *Next row* Beg at side edge rib 4 (6), cast off 2, rib until there are 7 sts on right needle after buttonhole, cast off 2, rib to end. On foll row cast on 2 sts over each buttonhole. Work 2 more rows in rib then cast off in rib.

▦ **Sleeves** With smaller needles and **A** cast on 37 (41) sts and work in rib for 9 (13) rows.

▦ *Inc row* Rib 4 (3), [inc in next st, rib 6] 4 (5) times, inc in next st, rib 4 (2). 42 (47) sts. Change to larger needles and working in st st work in stripe sequence but inc 1 st at both ends of every foll 6th row 10 times. Cont on 62 (67) sts until all the 68 (76) rows of patt have been completed. Cast off.

▦ **Neck Border** Join right shoulder seam. With right side of work facing and using smaller needles and **A**, pick up and k 43 (45) sts around front neck edge including edge of shoulder border and 36 (38) sts across back neck including edge of left shoulder border. Beg with 2nd row work in rib and after working 3 rows make buttonhole.

▦ *Next row* Rib 2, cast off 2, rib to end. On foll row cast on 2 sts over buttonhole. Work 2 more rows in rib then cast off in rib.

▦ **Finishing** Lap left front shoulder border over back border and oversew along side edges. Sew cast-off edge of sleeves to sides of armholes and sew armhole casting-off to last 4 rows on sides of sleeves. Join side and sleeve seams matching stripes. Sew buttons to left back shoulder border to correspond

with buttonholes.

BOOTEES

▦ **Left Foot** With larger needles and **A** cast on 45 sts and work in g st shaping at sides and centre.

▦ *1st and alt rows* K.

▦ *2nd row* K 1, k loop, k 21, k loop, k 1, k loop, k 21, k loop, k 1.

▦ *4th row* K 1, k loop, k 23, k loop, k 1, k loop, k 23, k loop, k 1. Cont to inc in these positions working 2 sts extra between incs each time, on next 3 alt rows. Work 8 rows on these 65 sts then shape instep.

▦ *1st row* (right side of work) K . 38, turn, leaving 27 sts unworked.

▦ *2nd row* K 11, turn, thus leaving 27 sts at this edge also.

▦ *3rd row* K 10, k 2 tog, turn. Rep 3rd row 23 times more, thus taking in 1 st extra from those at sides each time. Turn after last row and k to end; 41 sts rem. **

▦ *Next row* (wrong side) K 10 and leave these sts on a safety pin, cast off next 21 sts, k to end. Cont on 10 sts rem at end of needle and work 7 more rows in g st. Cast off. For ankle strap cast on 16 sts, take needle with these sts in right hand and beg at inner edge k across the other group of 10 sts. Cont on these 26 sts and work 3 rows then make buttonhole.

▦ *Next row* K 2, k 2 tog, yfd, k 22. Work 3 rows in g st then cast off. Fold cast-on edge in half and join with a flat seam. Join back seam of bootee. Sew button to side of ankle to correspond with buttonhole in strap.

▦ **Right Foot** Work as for left foot to **

▦ *Next row* (wrong side) K 10, turn and work a further 7 rows on these sts then cast off. Rejoin yarn to rem sts, cast off 21, k to end.

▦ Next row K 10, turn and cast on 16 sts for ankle strap. Cont on these 26 sts and work 3 rows.

▦ *Next row* K 22, yfd, k 2 tog, k 2. Work 3 more rows then cast off. Make up as for left foot; each bootee fastens at outside of foot.

▦ Work spots on instep of each bootee.

CALORIFIC COMFORT

Not the most suave and sophisticated of outfits, this cold weather combat suit is highly original and shows a strong sense of fun, as well as being comparatively easy to knit. It is also extremely practical: wide bands knitted in double-stranded yarn are alternated with narrow bands of single thickness, a design which guarantees thermal protection and comfort yet will keep its shape when washed.

CHECKLIST

Materials
Double knitting yarn: 14 (16) × 50g balls cream. Pair each of needles size 3mm, 3¾mm and 6mm; strip of elastic 2cm (¾in) wide for waist of trousers.

Sizes
Two sizes, to fit ages 9 to 12 (15 to 18) months. Actual measurements shown on diagram.

Stitches used
Single rib; g st; st st; k loop = pick up loop lying between needles and k it tbl; patt, worked as foll:
1st to 12th rows Work 12 rows in g st using yarn double stranded and 6mm needles.
13th to 16th rows Beg with a k row work 4 rows st st using yarn single-stranded and 3mm needles. These 16 rows form one patt.

Tension
Over patt 14 sts and 28 rows to 10cm (4in). Work a sample on 20 sts working 2 complete patts; when measuring the width tension, this must be done at centre of the g st band.

INSTRUCTIONS

SWEATER

Back With 3¾mm needles and single yarn cast on 45 (49) sts and work in rib.
1st row (right side) P 1, * k 1, p 1; rep from * to end.
2nd row K 1, * p 1, k 1; rep from * to end. Rep these 2 rows until work measures 4cm (1½in) ending with a 1st row.
Dec row Rib 5 (13), [p 2 tog, rib 6 (10)] 5 (3) times. 40 (46) sts. Now work in patt as given above and cont until 44 (52) rows have been worked in patt thus ending with 12th (4th) patt row.
Raglan Shaping *1st size only* Work the 4 st st rows without shaping then dec 1 st at both ends of next 6 alt rows; rep last 16 rows once. Cast off rem 16 sts for back neck.
2nd size only Dec 1 st at both ends of next 4 alt rows thus completing the g st section. Work the 4 st st rows without shaping then dec 1 st at both ends of next 6 alt rows; work the 4 st st rows without shaping then dec 1 st at both ends of next 4 alt rows. Cast off rem 18 sts for back neck.

Front Work as for back until 24 (28) rows of raglan shaping have been worked. 24 (26) sts.
Neck Shaping Rem rows are worked in g st with double-stranded yarn.
Next row K 9 and leave these sts of left front on a spare needle, cast off 6 (8), k to end. Cont on 9 sts now rem on needle for right front. ** Dec 1 st at neck edge on alt rows 3 times but *at same time* dec 1 st at raglan edge on next row and next 3 alt rows. Cast off rem 2 sts.
Rejoin yarn to neck edge of left front sts and complete as for right front from ** to end, reversing shapings.

Sleeves With 3¾mm needles and single yarn cast on 33 (37) sts and work in rib as on welt for 3(4)cm, 1⅛(1½)in, ending with a 1st rib row then work 1 more row working 1 dec at centre. 32 (36) sts.
Now work in patt but inc 1 st at both ends of every foll 8th (10th) row 6 times then cont on 44 (48) sts until 60 (68) rows have been worked in patt thus ending with 12th (4th) patt row.
Raglan Shaping Work as for correct size of back raglan but *at same time*, after 20 (24) rows of raglan have been worked, dec 1 st at centre of row on next row and next 5 alt rows, in addition to raglan shapings. When last raglan dec row has been worked cast off rem 14 sts.

Finishing and Neck Border Join front raglan seams and right back seam making neat backstitch seams and taking care to match patts. With right side of work facing and using 3¾mm needles and single yarn, pick up and k 11 sts across top of left sleeve, 21 (23) sts around front neck edge, 11 sts across top of right sleeve and 16 (18) sts across back neck. 59 (63) sts. Beg with 2nd row work in rib for 7 rows then cast off loosely in rib. Join left back raglan seam and ends of neck border. Join side and sleeve seams.

TROUSERS

Back This begins at waist

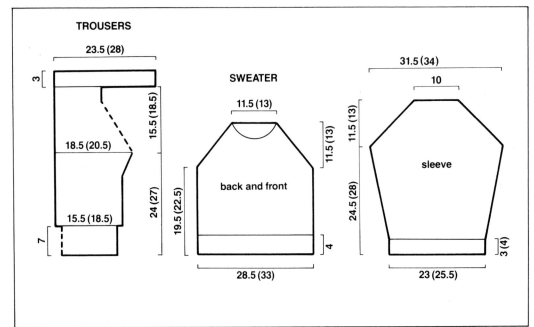

TROUSERS
23.5 (28)
3
15.5 (18.5)
18.5 (20.5)
15.5 (18.5)
24 (27)
7

SWEATER
11.5 (13)
11.5 (13)
11.5 (13)
24.5 (28)
19.5 (22.5)
back and front
28.5 (33)
4

31.5 (34)
10
sleeve
23 (25.5)
3 (4)

edge and is worked in one piece as far as crotch. With 3¾mm needles and single yarn cast on 43 (47) sts and work in rib as on sweater for 3cm (1⅛in) ending with a 1st rib row.

▦ *Dec row* Rib 3 (5), [p 2 tog, rib 2 (3)] 10 (8) times, rib 0 (2). 33 (39) sts. Now work in patt and cont until 12th row has been worked then begin centre shaping.

▦ *13th row* K 16 (19), k loop, k 1, k loop, k 16 (19). Cont to inc at each side of centre st on every foll 4th row 5 (9) times, then on every alt row 4 (0) times. Work 3 rows on these 53 (59) sts thus ending with 12th (4th) patt row. Divide legs as foll:

▦ *Next row* K 26 (29) and leave these sts on a spare needle, cast off 1, k to end. Cont on 26 (29) sts now rem on needle for one leg. Dec 1 st at inner leg next to opening on every foll 4th row 4 times then cont on rem 22 (25) sts until 92 (108) rows have been worked in patt from beg thus ending with a 12th patt row for both sizes. Cut yarn and leave sts on a piece of contrast yarn. With wrong side facing rejoin yarn to sts of other leg and complete in same way reversing shapings.

▢ **Front** Work as for back.

▦ **Finishing and Ankle Borders** Join side seams to within 2 rows of lower edges making neat backstitch seams and matching patt. With right side of work facing and using 3¾mm needles and single yarn work across the 2 groups of sts for right leg as foll: on back of leg k 7 (6), [k 2 tog, k 5 (4)] 2 (3) times, then k rem st tog with 1st st of front of leg, then [k 5 (4), k 2 tog] 2 (3) times, k 7 (6). Cont on these 39 (43) sts and beg with 2nd rib row work in rib for 7cm (2½in) then cast off loosely in rib. Work left ankle border in same way, beg at front. Join remainder of side seams at centre of ankle border. Join inner leg seams. Cut elastic to fit baby's waist, overlap ends forming a ring and sew securely. Attach elastic to inside of waistband with herringbone stitch.

LITTLE PRINCE

The simplest of stitches are used here with charming results: the open jacket, trousers, beret and socks are knitted almost entirely in garter stitch, with just a little double rib and stocking stitch on the beret. The fine soft yarn should lull even the most tender-skinned prince (or princess) to sleep. All these little garments are easy to make, including the socks, which are knitted on ordinary needles and have no complicated shaping.

CHECKLIST

Materials
Phildar Luxe 025: 5 × 50g balls peach for the set or, if made separately, 2 balls for the jacket, 2 balls for the trousers, 1 ball each for beret and socks. Pair of needles size 3¼mm; small size crochet hook.

Size
One size, to fit age birth to 3 months. Actual measurements shown on diagrams.

Stitches used
Double rib; g st; st st.

Tension
Over g st using 3¼mm needles, 23 sts and 46 rows to 10cm (4in). Work a sample on 28 sts; when counting rows each ridge that you can see counts as 2 rows.

INSTRUCTIONS

JACKET

Right Front Beg at lower edge cast on 24 sts and work in g st, counting 1st row as right side. Cont until work measures 13cm (5⅛in) from beg, ending with a right-side row. Cast on 36 sts for sleeve at beg of next row then cont on these 60 sts until work measures 18cm (7⅛in) from beg, ending at front edge.

Neck Shaping Cast off 3 sts at beg of next row, 2 sts at same edge on next alt row and 1 st on next 3 alt rows. Cont on rem 52 sts until work measures 21cm (8¼in) from beg, ending at neck edge after a wrong-side row. ** Cut yarn and leave sts on a spare needle. Work left front in same way but casting on sleeve sts at opposite edge and reversing neck shaping. Cont as for right front to ** but ending at side edge after a wrong-side row. This is the shoulder-line; place marker loops of contrast yarn at side edge of each section then cont for back.

Next row K 52 sts of left front, turn, cast on 16 sts, turn then beg at neck edge k 52 sts of right front. Cont on these 120 sts without shaping until work measures 8cm (3⅛in) from shoulder markers. Cast off 36 sts at beg of next 2 rows then cont on rem 48 sts and work 13cm (5⅛in). Cast off loosely.

Finishing Join side and sleeve seams, oversewing neatly and closely so that cuffs can be turned back if required. To neaten front and neck edges a row of slip-sts can be worked using a small size crochet hook.

TROUSERS

Back Beg at lower edge of one leg cast on 28 sts and work in g st counting 1st row as right side of main part. Dec 1 st at both ends of every foll 5th row 3 times then cont on rem 22 sts until work measures 10cm (4in) from beg, ending with a wrong-side row. Inc 1 st at beg of next row then at same edge on every foll 10th row twice more. Cont on these 25 sts until work measures 16cm (6¼in) from beg, ending at shaped edge

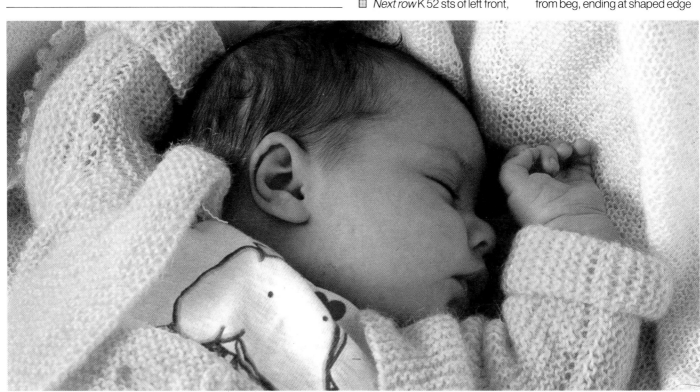

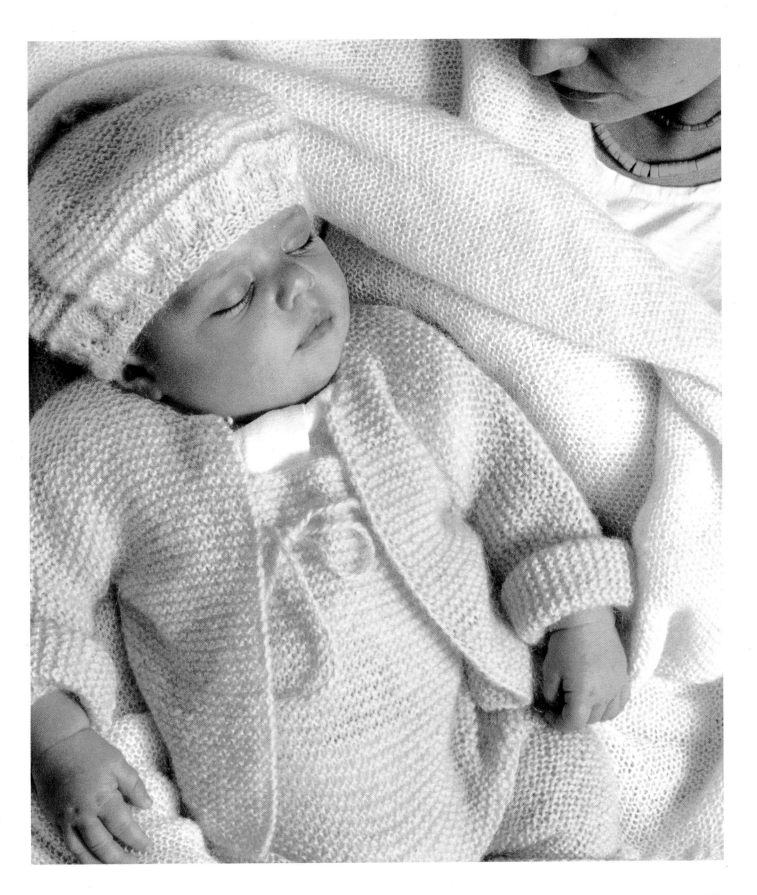

after a wrong side row. Cut yarn and leave sts on a spare needle. Work another piece in same way working the 3 leg incs at opposite edge. Cont until work is the same length as first leg, ending at outer edge after a wrong-side row.

▨ *Next row* K 25, turn, cast on 22 sts for gusset, turn, then k the 25 sts of first leg. K 1 row on these 72 sts then shape as foll:

▨ *1st row* K 24, SKPO, k 20, k 2 tog, k 24. Work 3 rows in g st.

▨ *5th row* K 24, SKPO, k 18, k 2 tog, k 24. Cont to dec in these positions on every foll 4th row 8 times more, working 2 sts fewer at centre each time. K 1 row on rem 52 sts.

▨ *39th row* K 25, k 2 tog, k 25. Cont on rem 51 sts until work measures 37cm (14½in) from beg then make a row of holes.

▨ *Next row* K 2, [yfd, k 2 tog, k 3] 9 times, yfd, k 2 tog, k 2. Work 9 more rows in g st then cast off rather loosely.

▨ **Front** Work as for back.

▨ **Finishing** Join side seams then join inner leg and gusset seam making neat oversewing seams so that legs can be turned up as shown. Make a length of crochet or twisted cord and thread through holes to fasten at front.

BERET

▨ Cast on 78 sts and work in double rib.

▨ *1st row* (right side) K 2, * p 2, k 2; rep from * to end.

▨ *2nd row* P 2, * k 2, p 2; rep from * to end. Rep these 2 rows once. Now work in st st and begin shaping.

▨ *1st row* K 2, [kfb, k 1] 38 times. P 1 row.

▨ *3rd row* K 2, [kfb, k 2] 38 times. Cont on these 154 sts and work 4 rows in st st.

▨ *8th row* K on wrong side. Work 2 more rows in st st. Now work in g st for crown and work 6 rows without shaping then shape top.

▨ *1st row* [K 17, k 2 tog] 8 times, k 2.

▨ *2nd and alt rows* K.

▨ *3rd row* [K 16, k 2 tog] 8 times, k 2.

▨ *5th row* [K 15, k 2 tog] 8 times, k 1. Cont to work 8 decs on every alt row working 1 st fewer before the dec each time, until 18 sts rem.

▨ *Next row* [K 2 tog] 9 times. Cut yarn leaving a long end, thread this through rem sts, draw up tightly and sew securely then use same length of yarn to backstitch seam. To make a little stalk for top of beret work a length of 7 ch using a small size crochet hook, miss 1st ch then work 1 d c in each rem ch. Fasten off and sew this stalk to top of beret.

SOCKS

▨ Cast on 28 sts for leg edge and work in g st until work measures 6cm (2⅜in) from beg then divide for heel. Cut yarn, slip off first 7 sts onto a holder, now slip next 14 sts which will form instep onto a double piece of contrast yarn, rejoin yarn and k

next 7 sts then onto same needle, beg at outer edge k the 7 sts from holder. The edges which will form back seam come at centre of these 14 sts. Cont in g st across all sts for 13 rows then shape heel.

▨ *1st row* K 9, k 2 tog, turn, thus leaving 3 sts unworked.

▨ *2nd row* K 5, k 2 tog, turn leaving 3 sts at this edge also. Rep 2nd row 6 times more thus taking in all the sts at sides; 6 sts rem.

▨ *Next row* K these 6 sts, then pick up and k 7 sts along side of heel, k the 14 sts of instep then pick up and k 7 sts along other side of heel. K 1 row on these 34 sts then begin shaping at sides of instep.

▨ *1st row* K 11, k 2 tog, k 14, SKPO, k 5.

▨ *2nd and alt rows* K.

▨ *3rd row* K 10, k 2 tog, k 14, SKPO, k 4.

▨ *5th row* K 9, k 2 tog, k 14, SKPO, k 3. Cont on rem 28 sts and work 3cm (1⅛in) without shaping, ending with a wrong-side row, then shape toe.

▨ *1st row* K 10, k 2 tog, k 10, SKPO, k 4.

▨ *2nd row* K.

▨ *3rd row* K 9, k 2 tog, k 10, SKPO, k 3.

▨ *4th row* K.

▨ *5th row* K 8, k 2 tog, k 10, SKPO, k 2.

▨ *6th row* K 1, k 2 tog, k 10, SKPO, k 7.

▨ *7th row* K 6, k 2 tog, k 10, SKPO.

▨ *8th row* [K 2 tog] 9 times. Cut yarn, pass end through rem sts, draw up tightly and sew securely. Make a neat flat seam along side of foot and backstitch seam along back of leg.

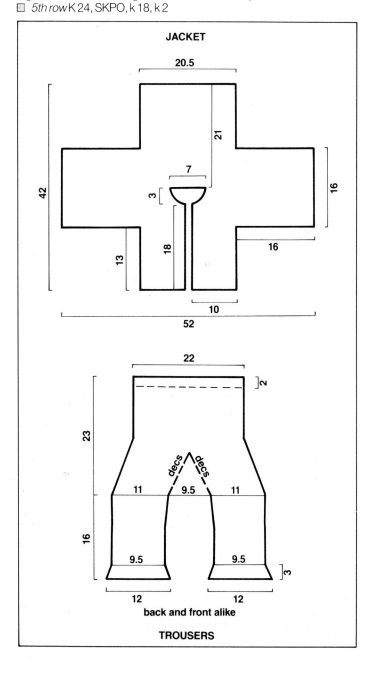

JACKET

20.5

21

7

3

42

16

18

13

16

10

52

22

2

23

decs decs

11   9.5   11

16

9.5   9.5

3

12   12

back and front alike

TROUSERS

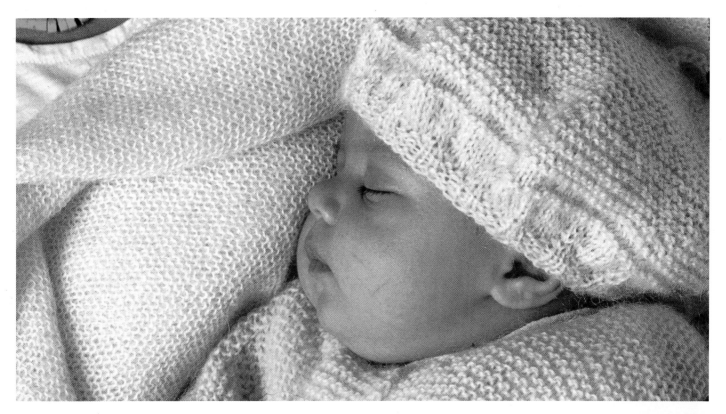

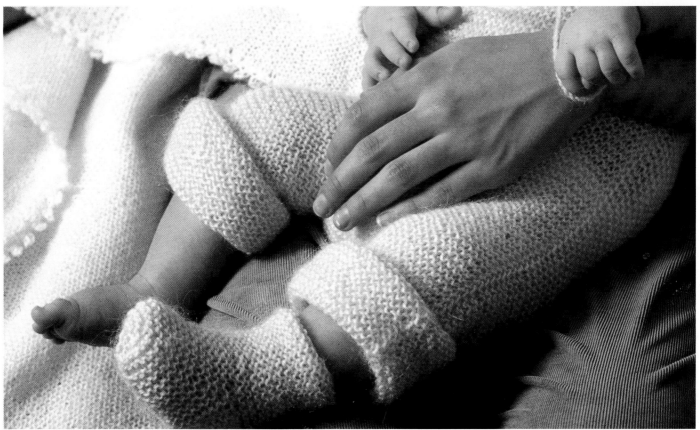

MIX AND MATCH SET

This wonderfully practical set, consisting of a sweater, rompers and matching bootees, is so quick and easy to knit that the temptation is to carry on knitting until you have several versions in different colourways, as here, for a versatile mix-and-match wardrobe. The sweater has a buttoned opening, worn either at the front or back, and is knitted in single yarn. For the rompers and bootees the yarn is used double stranded, to give extra firmness and warmth, and the only stitches used are stocking stitch, rib and garter stitch.

CHECKLIST

Materials
Phildar Prognostic 229: 2 × 50g balls white and 2 balls pink or other contrast colour for sweater; 12 balls pink or other colour for rompers, and one ball for bootees. Pair each of needles size 2¼mm, 2¾mm and 4½mm; 3 buttons for sweater, 2 large buttons for rompers, 2 small buttons for bootees.

Size
Two sizes, to fit ages 3 to 6 (9 to 12) months. Actual measurements of sweater and rompers are shown on diagram.

Stitches used
Single rib; st st; g st; k loop = pick up loop lying between needles and k it through the back.

Tension
Over st st and using 2¾mm needles and single yarn, 29 sts and 37 rows to 10cm (4in); work a sample on 35 sts. Over g st using 4½mm needles and double-stranded yarn, 17 sts and 34 rows to 10cm (4in); work a sample on 22 sts.

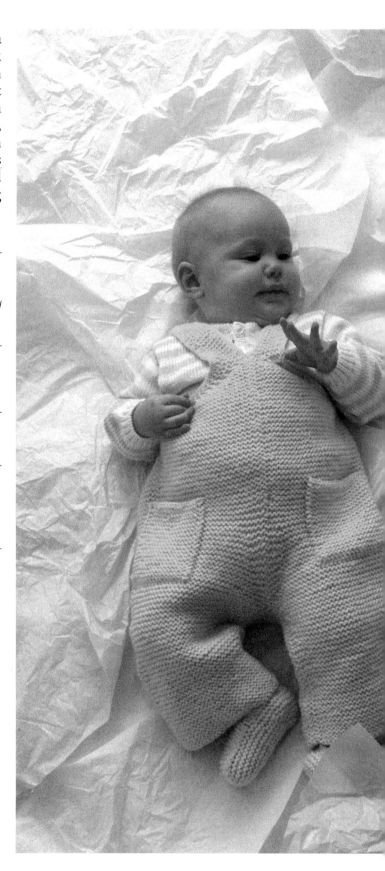

INSTRUCTIONS

SWEATER

▥ **Back** With 2¼mm needles and white, cast on 64 (70) sts and work in single rib for 8 rows. Change to 2¾mm needles and work in st st beg with a k row working stripes of 4 rows white, 4 rows pink (or other contrast colour) throughout. Cont until work measures 14(16)cm, 5½(6¼)in, from beg, ending with a p row.
▥ **Armhole Shaping** Cast off 5 sts at beg of next 2 rows. Work 2 (6) rows on rem 54 (60) sts.
▥ **Back Opening** *Next row* K 26 (29) and leave these sts of right back on a spare needle, cast off 2, k to end. Cont on 26 (29) sts

now rem on needle for left back, without shaping until work measures 24(27)cm, 9½(10⅝)in, from beg, ending at the opening edge.
▥ **Neck and Shoulder Shaping** Cast off for neck 10 (11) sts at beg of next row and 6 (7) sts at side edge of foll row. Cast off 3 sts at neck edge on next row then cast off rem 7 (8) sts to complete shoulder slope. Rejoin correct colour to sts of right back and complete as for left back reversing shapings.

▥ **Front** Work as for back until armhole shaping has been worked then cont on rem 54 (60) sts until work measures 20(23)cm, 7⅞(9)in, from beg, ending with a p row.

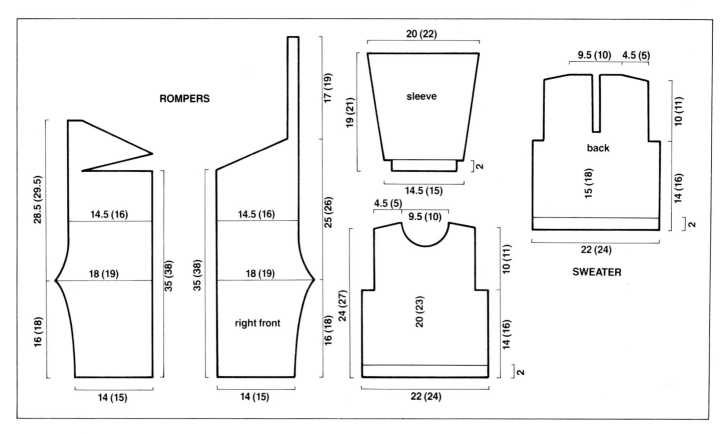

ROMPERS

28.5 (29.5)

14.5 (16)

18 (19)

16 (18)

35 (38)

14 (15)

35 (38)

14.5 (16)

18 (19)

right front

14 (15)

17 (19)

25 (26)

16 (18)

20 (22)

sleeve

19 (21)

14.5 (15)

2

4.5 (5)

9.5 (10)

24 (27)

20 (23)

14 (16)

22 (24)

10 (11)

2

9.5 (10)   4.5 (5)

back

15 (18)

22 (24)

SWEATER

10 (11)

14 (16)

2

■ **Neck and Shoulder Shaping** *1st row* K 23 (25) and leave these sts of left front on a spare needle, cast off next 8 (10) sts, k to end. Cont on 23 (25) sts now rem on needle for right front and work 1 row. ✳✳ Cast off 4 sts at beg of next row, 2 sts at same edge on next 2 alt rows and 1 st on next 2 alt rows. Cont on rem 13 (15) sts until work matches back to beg of shoulder, ending at side edge. Cast off 6 (7) sts at beg of next row, work 1 row then cast off rem 7 (8) sts.
■ Rejoin correct colour to neck edge of left front sts; complete as for right front from ✳✳ to end.

■ **Sleeves** With 2¼mm needles and white cast on 38 (40) sts and work 7 rows in single rib.
■ *Inc row* Rib 5 (6), [inc in next st, rib 8] 3 times, inc in next st, rib 5 (6). 42 (44) sts. Change to 2¾mm needles and work in striped st st as for back but inc 1 st at both ends of every foll 6th row 8 times (then at both ends of every foll 4th row twice for 2nd size). Cont on

58 (64) sts until work measures 19(21)cm, 7½(8¼)in, from beg. Cast off.

■ **Neck Border** First join shoulder seams. With right side of work facing and using 2¾mm needles and white, pick up and k 14 (15) sts across left back neck edge, 40 (42) sts around front neck and 14 (15) sts across right back neck. Work 4 rows in single rib then cast off loosely in rib.

■ **Back Borders** With right side of work facing and using 2¾mm needles and white, pick up and k 32 sts along left back edge of opening.
■ *1st row* ✳ K 1, p 1; rep from ✳ to end. Now make buttonholes.
■ *2nd row* Beg at base of opening rib 4, [yrn, p 2 tog, rib 10] twice, yrn, p 2 tog, rib 2. Work 1 more row then cast off in rib. Work similar border on right back edge of opening omitting buttonholes.

■ **Finishing** Sew cast-off edge of sleeves to sides of armholes

and sew armhole casting-off to a corresponding depth on sides of sleeves. Join side and sleeve seams matching stripes. Sew on buttons to correspond with buttonholes.

ROMPERS

Use double-stranded yarn throughout

■ **Right Front** With 4½mm needles cast on 24 (26) sts and work in g st counting 1st row as right side. Cont until work measures 4(6)cm, 1½(2⅜)in, from beg, ending with a wrong-side row. Shape inner edge of leg.
■ *1st row* K 3, k loop, k to end. Cont to inc in this position on every foll 6th row 4 times then on every foll 4th row twice. Cont on 31 (33) sts until work measures 16(18)cm, 6¼(7⅛)in, from beg, ending at shaped edge.
■ **Crotch Shaping** *1st row* K 3, k 2 tog, k to end. K 1 row then dec in same position on next row, then on every foll 4th row 4 times more. Cont on rem 25 (27) sts

until work measures 35(38)cm, 13¾(15)in, from beg, ending at shaped edge. ✳✳
■ **Armhole Shaping** *1st row* K to last 6 sts, SKTPO, k 3. Work the double dec in this position on every alt row 9 times more then cont on rem 5 (7) sts for shoulder strap; work 17(19)cm, 6¾(7½)in, then cast off.

■ **Left Front** Work leg section as for right front but working incs 3 sts in from the opposite edge. Cont on 31 (33) sts until work measures 16(18)cm, 6¼(7⅛)in, from beg, ending at straight side edge.
■ **Crotch Shaping** *1st row* K to last 5 sts, SKPO, k 3. Dec 1 st in same position on next alt row then on every foll 4th row 4 times more. Cont on rem 25 (27) sts until work measures 35(38)cm, 13¾(15)in, from beg, ending at straight side edge. ✳✳✳
■ **Armhole Shaping** *1st row* K 3, k 3 tog, k to end. Cont to work the double dec in this position on every alt row 9 times more then cont on rem 5 (7) sts and work

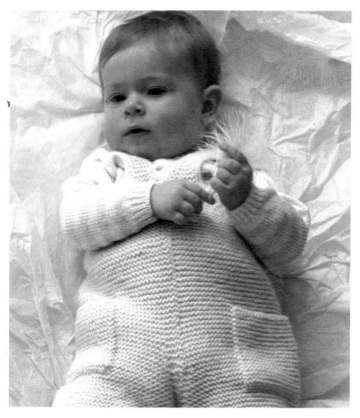

strap as for the right front.

■ **Right Back** Work as for left front to ✳✳✳ but ending at shaped edge then work shortened rows as foll:
■ *1st row* K 21 (23), turn.
■ *2nd and alt rows* K to end.
■ *3rd row* K 18 (20), turn.
■ *5th row* K 15 (17), turn. Cont to work 3 sts fewer before turning on next 3 alt rows; turn as usual and k to end. Work 1 row across all sts thus ending at side edge. Work armhole shaping as for left front and when shapings are completed cast off rem 5 (7) sts.

■ **Left Back** Work as for right front to ✳✳ thus ending at shaped edge. Work shortened rows as for right back until 2 rows have been worked on 6 (8) sts thus ending at shaped edge. Work armhole shaping as for right front and when shapings are completed cast off rem 5 (7) sts.

■ **Pockets** There are 2 pockets for front and 2 for back. With 4½mm needles cast on 16 (18)

sts for front pocket and work in g st for 8(9)cm, 3⅛(3½)in. Cast off.
■ Make another in same way.
■ For back pocket cast on 7 sts using 4½mm needles; work in g st but inc 1 st at both ends of every alt row 4 (5) times then cont on these 15 (17) sts until work measures 7(8)cm, 2¾(3⅛)in, from beg.
Cast off.
■ Make another pocket in same way.

■ **Finishing and Borders** Join side seams. With right side of work facing and using 2¼mm needles and yarn *single*, beg at centre back edge of left back pick up and k 124 (130) sts along entire left armhole edge and side of shoulder strap. Work 5 rows in g st then cast off rather tightly. Work similar border on right armhole beg at top of strap and ending at centre back. Join front seam. With right side facing and using 2¼mm needles and yarn *single*, pick up and k 108 (120) sts along inner edges of the 2

shoulder straps and work same border. Join centre back seam. Join inner leg seams.
■ Sew front pockets to fronts as shown. Sew back pockets approximately at centre of each back placing them 21(23)cm, 8¼(9)in, above cast-on edge of legs. Make a buttonhole loop at end of each shoulder strap and sew buttons to back to correspond.

BOOTEES

Use yarn double-stranded throughout.

■ With 4½mm needles cast on 26 (32) sts and work in g st, shaping both edges and centre.
■ *1st and alt rows* K.
■ *2nd row* K 1, k loop, k 11 (14), k loop, k 2, k loop, k 11 (14), k loop, k 1.
■ *4th row* K 1, k loop, k 13 (16), k loop, k 2, k loop, k 13 (16), k loop, k 1. Cont working incs in these positions working 2 extra sts between them on next 3 alt rows then cont on 46 (52) sts and work

6 rows without shaping.
■ **Instep Shaping** *1st row* K 27 (30), turn leaving 19 (22) sts unworked.
2nd row K 8, turn, leaving 19 (22) sts at this edge also.
3rd row K 7, k 2 tog, turn. Rep 3rd row 17 (19) times more thus taking in 1 st extra from those at sides on every row. Turn after last row and k to end. Cont on rem 28 (32) sts and work 4 rows across all sts. Cast off.
■ For ankle strap cast on 12 sts.
■ *1st row* K.
■ *2nd row* K 9, yfd, k 2 tog, k 1. K 1 row then cast off. Fold cast-on edge of bootee in half and sew with a flat seam. Sew back seam of bootee.
■ Sew ankle strap around front of leg section and sew on a button to correspond with buttonhole. When making 2nd bootee sew on strap the other way so that buttonhole of each bootee is at outside.

STYLISH STRIPES

A soft double knitting yarn and a brilliant colour scheme are used for this simple but stylish sweater, which is knitted entirely in garter stitch. It is made all in one piece and has a square neckline and a shoulder opening. The baby's snuggler with its matching stripe pattern provides delightful warmth without weight.

CHECKLIST

Materials

FOR THE SWEATER
*Double knitting yarn, one × 50g ball in each of the foll colours: turquoise (**A**), pale green (**B**), yellow (**C**), orange (**D**), delphinium blue (**E**), and raspberry red (**F**).*
Pair of needles size 4½mm.
2 buttons.

FOR THE SNUGGLER
*Double knitting yarn, 6 × 50g balls in each of the foll colours: turquoise (**A**), pale green (**B**), yellow (**C**), orange (**D**), delphinium blue (**E**), and raspberry red (**F**) as above.*
A long pair of needles size 6mm.

Sizes

Sweater, three sizes, to fit ages 3 (6-9) months. Actual measurements shown on diagram. Snuggler measures 81cm × 87cm (32in × 36in).

Stitches used

Each item is knitted entirely in g stitch.

Note *When making the snuggler, yarn is used double.*

Tension

Over g st using 4¼mm needles and yarn single, 19 sts and 38 rows to 10cm (4in). Work a sample on 24 sts. Over g st and using 6mm needles and yarn double, 16 sts and 26 rows to 10cm (4in). Work a sample on 20 sts.

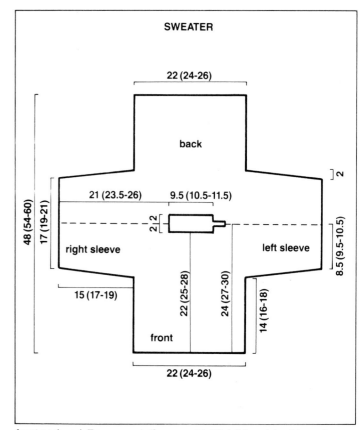

INSTRUCTIONS

SWEATER

▦ Each colour is used single.
▦ **Stripe sequence for sweater** Work 2 rows **C**, 2 rows **A**, 2 rows **D**, 2 rows **E**, 2 rows **F**, 2 rows **B**; rep these 12 rows 6(7-8) times more, then 2 rows **C**, 2 rows **A**, 2 rows **D**, 2 rows **E**. Now work 2 rows **F** at the shoulder line then cont for back working colours in reverse thus: 2 rows **E**, 2 rows **D**, 2 rows **A**, 2 rows **C**, then [2 rows **B**, 2 rows **F**, 2 rows **E**, 2 rows **D**, 2 rows **A**, 2 rows **C**] 7 (8-9) times.

▦ **To Make** Beg at lower edge of front cast on 42 (46-50) sts using 4½mm needles and **C**. Count 1st row as right side and work in stripe sequence as given above. Cont until 52 (60-68) rows have been worked.
▦ **Sleeve Shaping** Cast on 7 (8-9) sts at beg of next 8 rows. Cont on 98 (110-122) sts and work 24 (28-32) rows; 84 (96-108) rows have been worked in all.
▦ **Neck Shaping** *Next row* Using **C**, k 40 (45-50) and leave these sts of left front on a spare needle, cast off next 18 (20-22) sts, k to end. Cont on 40 (45-50) sts now rem on needle for right front and work 7 more rows thus completing stripe in **E**. Work 2 rows in **F** which form shoulder line then cont for right back and work next 8 rows thus ending at neck edge. Cut yarn and leave sts on a spare needle. With wrong side facing rejoin **C** to neck edge of left front sts and work 7 rows. Change to **F** for the shoulder line rows.
▦ *Next row* K 30 (35-40), cast off rem 10 sts at neck edge and fasten off. Onto free needle using **F** cast on 10 sts, take this needle in right hand and k across the 30 (35-40) sts. Now cont for left back and work 8 rows thus completing a stripe in **C**.
▦ *Next row* With **B**, k the 40 (45-50) sts of left back, turn, cast on 18 (20-22) sts, turn then onto same needle k the 40 (45-50) sts of right back. Cont on these 98 (110-122) sts and work 23 (27-31) rows.
▦ **Sleeve Shaping** Cast off 7 (8-9) sts at beg of next 8 rows. Cont on rem 42 (46-50) sts and work 52 (60-68) rows thus completing all stripes. Cast off.

▦ **Finishing** Join side and sleeve seams, matching stripes. Make 2 buttonhole loops on front edge of left shoulder opening and sew buttons to left back shoulder to correspond.

SNUGGLER

▦ Each colour is used double. Wind a ball into 2 equal balls and rewind these tog to form a double-stranded ball which will be easier to use. Cut off each colour on completion of stripe.
▦ With 6mm needles and **A** cast on 129 sts and working in g st work 2 rows **A**, 2 rows **E**, 2 rows **C**, 2 rows **B**, 2 rows **D**, 2 rows **F**. Cont to rep these 12 rows until 226 rows have been worked. Cast off.

APRIL TWOSOME

For days with just a hint of warmth, here is a pretty little outfit as fresh and welcome as fruit blossom. The button-up cardigan and skirt are knitted in a soft mohair yarn and have a pattern of eyelet holes, with a line of zigzags across the yoke and below the skirt waistband. The cardigan has raglan armholes and the skirt finishes with a deep band of ribbing and an elasticated waist.

CHECKLIST

Materials

Pingouin Calin: 4 (5-6) × 50g balls white for the set. Pair each of needles size 2¾mm and 3mm; 6 buttons; narrow elastic for skirt.

Sizes

Three sizes, to fit ages 12 months (2-3 years). Actual measurements shown on diagram.

Stitches used

Single rib; eyelet patt, *worked on a multiple of 5 sts plus 1 as foll:*
    1st row *K.*
    2nd and alt rows *P.*
    3rd row ** K 3, k 2 tog, yfd; * rep from * to * ending k 1.*
    5th row *K.*
    7th row *K 1, * k 2 tog, yfd, k 3; * rep from * to *.*
    8th row *P. These 8 rows form one patt.*
For the zig-zag lace patt see instructions for each section.

Tension

Over patt using 3mm needles, 26 sts and 38 rows to 10cm (4in). Work a sample on 31 sts.

INSTRUCTIONS

CARDIGAN

⊞ **Back** With smaller needles, cast on 71 (81-91) sts and work in rib.
⊞ *1st row* (right side) P 1, * k 1, p 1; rep from * to end.
⊞ *2nd row* K 1, * p 1, k 1; rep from * to end. Rep these 2 rows 5 times more. Change to larger needles and work in eyelet patt as given above. Cont until work measures 19(21-23)cm, 7½(8¼-9)in, from beg, ending with a p row.
⊞ **Raglan Shaping** Cast off 2 sts at beg of next 2 rows, work 1 row then dec 1 st at both ends of foll row. Now begin zig-zag lace patt.
⊞ *1st row* K 5, * k 2 tog, yfd, k 1, yfd, SKPO, k 5; * rep from * to *.
⊞ *2nd row* P.
⊞ *3rd row* K 4, * k 2 tog, yfd, k 3, yfd, SKPO, k 3; * rep from * to * ending k 1.
⊞ *4th row* P 2 tog, p to last 2 sts, p 2 tog.
⊞ *5th row* K 2, * k 2 tog, yfd, k 5, yfd, SKPO, k 1; * rep from * to * ending k 1.
⊞ *6th row* P.
⊞ *7th row* K 1, k 2 tog, * yfd, k 7, yfd, SKTPO; * rep from * to * ending yfd, k 7, yfd, SKPO, k 1.
⊞ *8th row* As 4th. 61 (71-81) sts. This completes zig-zag patt. Cont in st st and dec 1 st at both ends of every foll 4th row 5 times, then at both ends of every alt row 4 times then at both ends of every row 10 (14-18) times. Cast off rem 23 (25-27) sts for back neck.

⊞ **Right Front** With smaller needles cast on 43 (49-53) sts and work in rib as on back welt for 6 rows then make buttonhole.
⊞ *7th row* Rib 3, cast off 3, rib to end. On foll row cast on 3 sts over buttonhole. Work 3 more rows in rib thus ending at side edge.
⊞ *12th row* For 1st size rib 17, inc in next st, rib 17 (for 2nd size rib 41 without inc; for 3rd size rib 22, inc in next st, rib 22), then for all sizes turn leaving 8 sts at front edge unworked and place these sts onto a safety pin for border to be worked later. Cont on rem 36 (41-46) sts; change to larger needles and work in eyelet patt until 1 more row has been worked than on back to beg of raglan shaping thus ending at side.
⊞ **Raglan Shaping** Cast off 2 sts at beg of next row, work 1 row then dec 1 st at beg of foll row. 33 (38-43) sts. Now work band of zig-zag lace patt.
⊞ *1st row* For 1st size: k 3, then rep from * to * in 1st row of this patt on back 3 times (for 2nd size k 1, yfd, SKPO, k 5, then rep from * to * in 1st row of this patt 3 times; for 3rd size k 3, then rep from * to * in 1st row of this patt 4 times).
⊞ *2nd row* P.
⊞ *3rd row* For 1st size k 2, then rep from * to * in 3rd row of this patt 3 times, k 1 (for 2nd size k 2, yfd, SKPO, k 3, then rep from * to * in 3rd row of this patt 3 times, k 1; for 3rd size k 2, then rep from * to * in 3rd row of this patt 4 times, k 1).
⊞ *4th row* P 2 tog, p to end.
⊞ *5th row* For 1st size k 1, then rep from * to * in 5th row of this patt 3 times, k 1 (for 2nd size k 3, yfd, SKPO, k 1, then rep from * to * in 5th row of this patt 3 times, k 1; for 3rd size k 1, then rep from * to * in 5th row of this patt 4 times, k 1).
⊞ *6th row* P.
⊞ *7th row* K 9 (4-9), yfd, SKTPO, rep from * to * in 7th row of this patt once (twice-twice), yfd, k 7, yfd, SKPO, k 1.
⊞ *8th row* As 4th. 31 (36-41) sts. Now work in st st and dec 1 st at raglan edge on every foll 4th row 5 times, then at same edge on

every alt row 4 times, then dec 1 st at same edge on every row 0 (4-6) times; 22 (23-26) sts rem, ending at front edge.
⊞ **Neck Shaping** Cast off 4 (5-5) sts at beg of next row, 2 sts at same edge on next 2 alt rows and 1 st on next 2 (2-3) alt rows; *at same time*, cont to dec at raglan edge on next 10 (10-12) rows. Cast off rem 2 sts.

⊞ **Left Front** With smaller needles cast on 43 (49-53) sts and work in rib as on back for 11 rows.
⊞ *12th row* Rib 8 and slip these sts onto a safety pin for border, then for 1st size rib 17, inc in next st, rib 17 (for 2nd size rib 41 without inc; for 3rd size rib 22, inc in next st, rib 22). Change to larger needles and cont on these 36 (41-46) sts; work in eyelet patt until you have worked same number of rows as on back up to raglan thus ending at side edge.
⊞ **Raglan Shaping** Cast off 2 sts at beg of next row, work 2 rows straight then dec 1 st at same edge on foll row. Now work band of zig-zag lace patt.
⊞ *1st row* For 1st and 3rd sizes, k 5, then rep from * to * in 1st row of this patt instead of k 3 (for 2nd size k 5, rep from * to * in 1st row of this patt 3 times, k 2 tog, yfd, k 1).
⊞ *2nd row* P.
⊞ *3rd row* For 1st and 3rd sizes, k 4, rep from * to * in 3rd row of this patt ending last rep k 2 instead of k 3 (for 2nd size k 4, rep from * to * in 3rd row of this patt 3 times, k 2 tog, yfd, k 2).
⊞ *4th row* P to last 2 sts, p 2 tog.
⊞ *5th row* For all sizes, k 2, rep from * to * in 5th row of this patt 3 (3-4) times (for 2nd size only, k 2 tog, yfd, k 3).
⊞ *6th row* P.
⊞ *7th row* K 1, k 2 tog, rep from * to * in 7th row of this patt 2 (3-3) times, yfd, k 9 (4-9).
⊞ *8th row* As 4th. 31 (36-41) sts. Cont in st st and complete as for right front reversing shapings.

⊞ **Sleeves** With smaller needles cast on 33 (37-39) sts and work in rib for 4cm (1½in) ending with a 1st rib row.

Inc row Rib 2 (2-3), [inc in next st, rib 3 (3-2)] 7 (8-11) times, inc in next st, rib 2. 41 (46-51) sts. Change to larger needles and work in eyelet patt but inc 1 st at both ends of 4th row then every foll 6th row 9 (10-11) times working extra sts into patt. Cont on 61 (68-75) sts until work measures 21(23-25)cm, 8¼(9-9¾)in, from beg, ending with a p row.

Raglan Shaping Cont in patt for remainder of sleeve; cast off 2 sts at beg of next 2 rows, dec 1 st at both ends of next alt row, then every foll 4th row 6 times, then dec at both ends of every alt row 6 (7-8) times after which dec 1 st at both ends of next 10 (12-14) rows. Cast off rem 11 (12-13) sts.

Front Borders Using smaller needles cast on 1 st, take needle with this st in right hand and beg at inner edge next to main part work in rib across sts of left front border. Cont in rib on these 9 sts until border when slightly stretched fits along front edge to neckline, ending with a 2nd rib row. Cut yarn and leave sts on a safety pin. Work right front border in same way but making 4 more buttonholes each 5.5(6-6.5)cm, 2⅛(2⅜-2½)in, above cast-off edge of previous one then cont until border is same length as left front border ending with a 2nd rib row. Leave sts on a safety pin but do not cut yarn.

Finishing and Neck Border Join raglan seams, Sew on front borders stretching them slightly to fit. With right side facing and using smaller needles, rib sts of right front border, pick up and k 15 (16-18) sts around right front neck edge, 9 (10-11) sts across right sleeve top, 23 (25-27) sts across back neck, 9 (10-11) sts across left sleeve top and 15 (16-18) sts around left front neck edge then rib 9 sts of front border. 89 (95-103) sts. Beg with 2nd row cont in rib across all sts and after working 1 row make another buttonhole at right front edge on next 2 rows. Rib 3 more rows then cast off in rib. Join side

and sleeve seams. Sew on buttons to correspond with buttonholes.

SKIRT

◫ **Back** With smaller needles cast on 125 (141-155) sts and work 2 rows in rib but inc 1 st at end of 2nd row on 1st and 3rd sizes. 126 (141-156) sts. Change to larger needles and work in eyelet patt; work 8 rows then shape to form curved edge as foll:

◫ *1st row* K 111 (126-141), turn.

◫ *2nd row* P 96 (111-126), turn. Keeping patt correct work 15 sts fewer before turning on each of next 6 rows. Turn after last row and k to end. Now work across all sts in patt until work measures 15(18-21)cm, 5⅞(7⅛-8¼)in, from beg, measured at centre, ending with a p row and working 1 dec at end of last row for 1st and 3rd sizes. 125 (141-155) sts. Now work band of zig-zag lace.

◫ *1st row* K 5 (8-5), * k 2 tog, yfd, k 1, yfd, SKPO, k 5; * rep from * to * ending last rep k 5 (8-5).

◫ *2nd and alt rows* P.

◫ *3rd row* K 4 (7-4), * k 2 tog, yfd, k 3, yfd, SKPO, k 3; * rep from * to * ending last rep k 4 (7-4) instead of k 3.

◫ *5th row* K 3 (6-3), * k 2 tog, yfd, k 5, yfd, SKPO, k 1; * rep from * to * 11 (12-14) times more, k 2 (5-2).

◫ *7th row* K 2 (5-2), k 2 tog, * yfd, k 7, yfd, SKTPO; rep from * to * 10 (11-13) times more, yfd, k 7, yfd, SKPO, k 2 (5-2).

◫ *8th row* For 1st size, p 4, [p 2 tog, p 3] 24 times, p 1 (for 2nd size p 5, [p 2 tog, p 2, p 2 tog, p 3] 15 times, p 1; for 3rd size p 6, [p 2 tog, p 2] 36 times, p 5).

◫ *All sizes* Cont on rem 101 (111-119) sts; change to smaller needles and work in rib for 6cm (2½in) ending with a 1st rib row. K 1 row on wrong side to make a ridge for fold-line then beg with 1st rib row work a further 7 rows in rib for hem. Cast off loosely in rib.

◫ **Front** Work exactly as for back.

◫ **Finishing** Join side seams. Cut elastic to child's waist measurement, overlap ends to form a ring and sew securely. Fold hem section to inside along the foldline enclosing elastic and slip-st cast-off edge loosely in place.

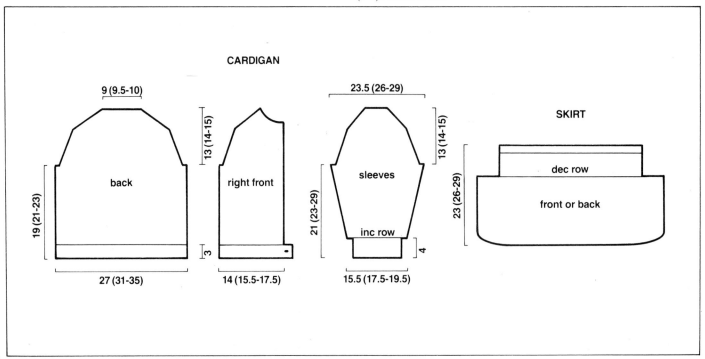

CARDIGAN

9 (9.5-10)

13 (14-15)

back

right front

19 (21-23)

3

27 (31-35)

14 (15.5-17.5)

23.5 (26-29)

13 (14-15)

sleeves

inc row

21 (23-29)

4

15.5 (17.5-19.5)

SKIRT

dec row

front or back

23 (26-29)

ANIMAL MAGIC

Children adore to dress up and have a natural love of animals, so they will instantly feel part of the animal kingdom when they wear these charming and imaginative sweaters, with their animal faces and matching hoods. The crafty fox and the gentle lamb, the mischievous mouse and the clever cat – for once they can all live together in harmony in a happy world of make-believe. All the designs are easy and quick to knit, using only simple stitches.

CHECKLIST

Materials
Fox *Wendy Mohair 90: 4 (4-5) × 50g balls rust (**A**), 25 (30-35)g white (**B**). Small amount of 4-ply yarn in black for nose. Pair each of needles size 4mm and 5½mm; 2 buttons to fasten; 4 buttons for eyes.*

Lamb *Wendy Mohair 90: 5 (6-7) × 50g balls white (**A**), and one ball peach (**B**). Pair each of needles size 6½mm and 9mm; 2 buttons to fasten; 4 buttons for eyes; deeper peach yarn for embroidery on the nose.*

Mouse *Wendy Mohair 90: 4(4-5) × 50g balls pink (**A**), one ball grey (**B**). Pair each of needles size 4mm and 5½mm; 2 buttons to fasten; 4 buttons for eyes; russia braid for whiskers; scrap of dress stiffening for teeth; yarn for embroidery.*

Cat *Wendy Mohair 90: 2 × 50g balls grey (**A**), 3 balls white (**B**). Pair each of needles size 4mm and 5½mm; 2 buttons to fasten; 4 buttons for eyes; russia braid for whiskers; pink yarn for nose.*

Sizes
Sweaters each have the same shape and are in three sizes, to fit ages 2 (4-6) years. Actual measurements shown on diagram.
Hoods are in one size, to fit a child of about 4 to 6 years. The hoods vary slightly in shape and are shown on separate diagrams.

Stitches used
Single rib; g st; st st.

Tensions
Over g st using 5½mm needles and yarn single, 15 sts and 28 rows to 10cm (4in). Work a sample on 13 sts.
Over st st using 5½mm needles and yarn single, 15 sts and 22 rows to 10cm (4in). Work a sample on 20 sts.
Over g st using 9mm needles and yarn double, 9 sts and 14 rows to 10cm (4in). Work a sample on 13 sts.

INSTRUCTIONS

FOX

▦ **Sweater Back** With smaller needles and **A** cast on 47 (49-53) sts and work in rib.
▦ ****** *1st row* (right side) P 1, * k 1, p 1; rep from * to end.
▦ *2nd row* K 1, * p 1, k 1; rep from * to end. Rep these 2 rows until work measures 4cm (1½in) from beg, ending with a 2nd rib row (but for 2nd size inc 1 st in centre of last row). ******.
▦ Change to larger needles and cont on 47 (50-53) sts working in g st. Cont until work measures 18(20-22)cm, 7⅛(7⅞-8⅝)in, from beg.

72

■ **Armhole Shaping** Cast off 4 sts at beg of next 2 rows then cont on rem 39 (42-45) sts until work measures 33(36-39)cm, 13(14⅛-/15⅜)in, from beg. Cast off all sts for shoulders and back neck.

■ **Front** Work as for back until work measures 26(29-32)cm, 10¼(11⅜-12⅝)in, from beg, ending with a wrong-side row.
■ **Neck Shaping** *1st row* K 17 (18-19) and leave these sts of left front on a spare needle, cast off next 5 (6-7) sts, k to end. Cont on 17 (18-19) sts now rem on needle for right front. ✳✳✳ Dec 1 st at neck edge on next 4 rows then at same edge on next 3 alt rows. Cont on rem 10 (11-12) sts until work matches back to shoulder edge. Cast off. Rejoin yarn to neck edge of left front sts and complete as for right front from ✳✳✳ to end reversing shapings.

■ **Sleeves** With smaller needles and **A** cast on 31 (33-37) sts and work as for back welt from ✳✳ to ✳✳. 31 (34-37) sts. Change to larger needles and work in g st but inc 1 st at both ends of every foll 6th (6th-7th) row 8 times. Cont on 47 (50-53) sts until work measures 26(28-30)cm, 10¼(11-11¾)in, from beg. Cast off.

■ **Finishing and Neck Border** On cast-off edge of back mark centre 19 (20-21) sts which will form neckline, leaving 10 (11-12) sts each side for shoulders. Join right shoulder seam. With right side of work facing and using smaller needles and **A**, pick up and k 41 (43-45) sts around front neck edge and 24 (24-26) sts across back neck. 65 (69-71) sts. Beg with 2nd row work 6 rows in rib as on welt then cast off in rib. Join right shoulder seam for the first 3 (4-5) sts from side edges. Along rem edge of front work 2 buttonhole loops, one near to neck edge and the other half-way along. Sew buttons to back shoulder to correspond. Sew cast-off edge of sleeves to sides of armholes and sew armhole casting-off to a corresponding depth on sides of sleeves. Join side and sleeve seams.

▦ **Pocket** With larger needles and **A** cast on 3 sts for lower point; the nose is worked later. Work in st st but inc 1 st at both ends of 3rd row, work 4 rows straight, inc 1 st at both ends of next row and next 3 (4-5) alt rows. Cont on 13 (15-17) sts until work measures 10(11-11)cm, 4(4¼-4¼)in, from beg. Cast off.

▦ For nose use the black 4-ply yarn double; cast on 3 sts using larger needles and work in st st. Inc 1 st at both ends of 2nd row then work 3 rows straight. Cast off. With p side of nose to k side of pocket slip-st nose to lower point.

▦ With right side of work facing and using larger needles and **B**, pick up and k 15 (17-17) sts along one side edge of pocket. Rep 2nd rib row then keeping rib correct

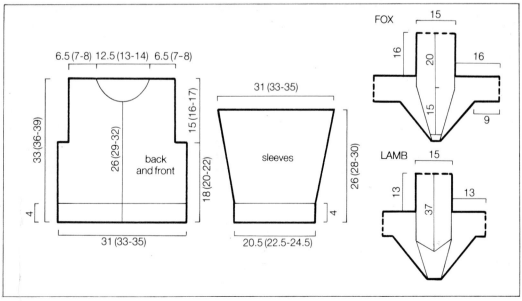

dec 1 st at lower edge of next 3 rows. Cast off in rib. Work similar border along other side edge.

▦ **Ears** For outer section cast on 3 sts using larger needles and **A**. Work in rib but inc 1 st at both ends of every alt row 4 times then work 4 rows straight. Cast off in rib.

▦ For inner section cast on 3 sts using larger needles and **B** work in rib, inc 1 st at both ends of every alt row 3 times then work 4 rows straight. Cast off in rib. Placing cast-off edges level sew outer and inner sections tog neatly. Sew ears to top of pocket and sew on eyes. Sew pocket to centre front just above welt.

▦ **Hood** For centre section cast on 3 sts using larger needles and **A**. Work in st st but inc 1 st at both ends of 2nd row, work 4 rows straight then inc 1 st at both ends of next row, then every foll 3rd row 8 times more. Cont on these 23 sts and work 20cm (7⅞in) without shaping, ending with a p row. Cut yarn and leave sts on a holder. Work nose as for pocket but after the inc row work 4 rows straight then cast off these 5 sts.

▦ Sew nose to lower point of hood in same way as for pocket. On left side edge of centre section mark off the first 19cm (7½in). With right side of work facing and using larger needles and **A**, pick up and k 39 sts on marked section. Rep 2nd rib row then keeping rib correct dec 1 st at lower edge on next 20 rows. Cont on rem 19 sts until work measures 16cm (6¼in) measured along straight side edge, ending with a wrong-side row. Cut yarn and leave sts on a holder.

▦ Work similar border along right side edge of centre section, reversing shapings; when work is same length as first side, ending with a wrong-side row, cont as foll. Work in rib across 19 sts of this side section, cont in rib across 23 sts of centre section then rib sts of first side section. 61 sts. Change to **A** and cont in rib across all sts for 9cm (3½in). Cast off in rib.

▦ **Ears** For outer section cast on

3 sts using larger needles and **A**. Work in rib but inc 1 st at both ends of every alt row 6 times. Work 2 rows on these 15 sts then cast off in rib.

▦ For inner section cast on 3 sts using larger needles and **B**. Work in rib but inc 1 st at both ends of every alt row 5 times. Work 1 row on these 13 sts then cast off in rib. Placing cast-off edges level sew inner section to outer section.

▦ **Finishing** Join back seams of hood and make a neat backstitch seam at centre front. Sew ears to top of hood. Sew on buttons for eyes.

LAMB

▦ Use yarn double throughout.
▦ **Sweater Back** With smaller needles and **A** cast on 29 (31-33) sts and work in rib as for Fox; cont until work measures 4cm (1½in) from beg, ending with a 2nd rib row. Change to larger needles and work in g st. Cont until work measures 18(20-22)cm, 7⅛(7⅞-8⅝)in, from beg.
▦ **Armhole Shaping** Cast off 3 sts at beg of next 2 rows then cont on rem 23 (25-27) sts until work measures 33(36-39)cm, 13(14⅛-15⅜)in, from beg. Cast off all sts for shoulder and back neck edges.

▦ **Front** Work as for back until you have worked 9 rows fewer than on back.
▦ **Neck Shaping** *1st row* K 10 (11-11) and leave these sts on a spare needle, cast off next 3 (3-5) sts, k to end. Cont on 10 (11-11) sts now rem on needle. Dec 1 st at neck edge on next 3 rows then at same edge on next alt row. Work 3 rows on rem 6 (7-7) sts then cast off these sts for shoulder edge. Rejoin yarn to neck edge of first group of sts and complete in same way, reversing neck shapings.

▦ **Sleeves** With smaller needles and **A** cast on 17 (19-21) sts and work in rib for 4cm (1½in) but inc 1 st in centre of last row. 18 (20-22) sts. Change to larger needles and work in g st but inc 1 st at both ends of every foll 4th (4th-5th) row 5 times. Cont on 28 (30-32) sts

until work measures 26(28-30)cm, 10¼(11-11¾)in, from beg. Cast off all sts.

▦ **Finishing and Neck Border** On cast-off edge of back mark centre 11 (11-13) sts for neckline leaving 6 (7-7) sts on each side for shoulders. Join right shoulder seam. With right side of work facing and using smaller needles and **A**, pick up and k 28 (28-30) sts around front neck edge and 15 (15-17) sts across back neck. 43 (43-47) sts. Beg with 2nd row work 4 rows in rib then cast off in rib. Work remainder of making up as for Fox.

▦ **Pocket** With smaller needles and **B** cast on 5 (5-7) sts and work in st st. Inc 1 st at both ends of 2nd row then cont on 7 (7-9) sts until work measures 6(6-7)cm, 2⅜(2⅜-2¾)in, from beg, ending with a p row. Now form point in **A** at centre.
▦ *1st row* K 3 (3-4) **B**, join on small ball of **A**, k 1 **A**, then 3 (3-4) **B**.
▦ *2nd row* P 2 (2-3) **B**, twist yarns, p 3 **A**, join on a small ball of **B**, p 2 (2-3) **B**. Always twisting yarns when changing colour work 2 extra sts in **A** at centre on next 2 (2-3) rows. Cast off all sts.

▦ **Ears** For outer section cast on 3 (3-5) sts using smaller needles and **A**. Work in rib but inc 1 st at

both ends of every alt row twice then work 4 rows on these 7 (7-9) sts. Cast off in rib. For inner section cast on 3 (3-5) sts using smaller needles and **B**. Work in rib but inc 1 st at both ends of every alt row twice. Work 2 rows on these 7 (7-9) sts then cast off in rib.
▦ Placing cast-off edges level sew inner and outer sections neatly tog. Sew ears to top of pocket and sew on eyes.
▦ Embroider the nose with a deeper peach colour. Sew the pocket to centre front just above welt.

▦ **Hood** Tension for this, working in st st on smaller needles is 11 sts and 14 rows to 10cm (4in).
▦ For centre section cast on 5 sts using smaller needles and **B**. Work in st st and inc 1 st at both ends of 3rd row, work 7 rows straight then inc 1 st at both ends of next row. 9 sts. Now begin forming point in **A** at centre.
▦ *12th row* P 4 **B**, join on a ball of **A**, p 1 **A**, then p 4 **B**.
▦ *13th row* K 3 **B**, twist yarns, k 3 **A**, join on a small ball of **B**, k 3 **B**.
▦ *14th row* P 2 **B**, twist yarns, p 5 **A**, 2 **B**. Inc 1 st at both ends of next row, then every foll 4th row 3 times more but *at same time* cont to work 2 extra sts in **A** at centre until all sts are in **A**. When incs are completed cont on these 17 sts and work 18cm (7⅛in) without shaping, ending with a p row. Cut

yarn and leave sts on a holder.

On each side edge mark a point 20cm (7⅞in) from beg. With right side of work facing and using smaller needles and **A**, pick up and k 29 sts along this marked section on left side. Rep 2nd rib row then keeping rib correct dec 1 st at lower edge on next 18 rows. Cont on rem 11 sts until work measures 13cm (5⅛in) along straight side edge, ending with a wrong-side row. Cut yarn and leave sts on a holder. Work similar border along right side edge of centre, reversing shapings, and when this section measures same length as first section ending with a wrong-side row cont as foll: work in rib across these 11 sts, cont in rib across 17 sts of centre section then cont in rib across 11 sts of first side section. 39 sts. Cont across all sts in rib for 10cm (4in). Cast off in rib.

Ears For outer section cast on 5 sts using smaller needles and **A**; work in rib but inc 1 st at both ends of every alt row 3 times then cont on 11 sts until work measures 13cm (5⅛in) from beg. Cast off in rib.

For inner section cast on 5 sts using smaller needles and **B**. Work in rib but inc 1 st at both ends of 3rd row then cont on these 7 sts until work measures 11cm (4¼in) from beg. Cast off in rib.

Finishing Placing cast-off edges level sew inner and outer sections of ears neatly tog. Join back seams of hood and join ribbed section with a neat backstitch join at centre front. Sew ears to top of hood. Embroider nose with deeper peach shade. Sew on eyes.

MOUSE

Sweater For back, front and sleeves work as for sweater of Fox design but using col **A** (pink).

Finishing and Neck Border As for Fox sweater.

Pocket With larger needles and **B** cast on 4 (5-6) sts and work in st st but inc 1 st at both ends of

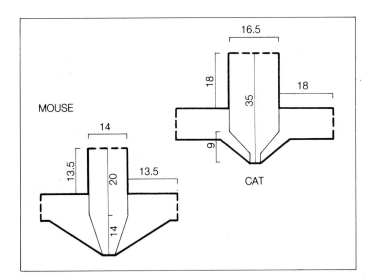

MOUSE

CAT

every alt row 6 times. Cont on 16 (17-18) sts until work measures 9(9-10)cm, 3½(3½-4)in, from beg. Cast off. With right side facing and using larger needles and **B**, pick up and k 15 (15-17) sts along one side edge of pocket. Rep 2nd rib row then keeping rib correct dec 1 st at lower edge on next 3 rows. Cast off in rib. Work similar border on other side.

■ **Ears** With larger needles and **B** cast on 3 (3-5) sts for outer section and work in rib. Inc 1 st at both ends of every alt row 3 times then work 6 rows on these 9 (9-11) sts. Cast off in rib. For inner section cast on 3 (3-5) sts using larger needles and **A**. Work in rib but inc 1 st at both ends of every alt row 3 times then work 3 rows on these 9 (9-11) sts. Cast off in rib.

■ Placing cast-on and cast-off edges level sew inner and outer sections neatly tog. Sew ears to top of pocket. Sew pocket to centre front just above welt. Cut whiskers and pass through base of pocket. Cut out teeth from stiffened fabric and sew in place. Embroider nose in black yarn. Sew eyes in place.

■ **Hood** With larger needles and **B** cast on 3 sts for centre section and work in st st; inc 1 st at both ends of every foll 3rd row 5 times then every foll 4th row 4 times. Cont on these 21 sts until work measures 34cm (13⅜in) from beg, ending with a p row. Cut yarn

and leave sts on a holder. On each side edge mark a point 20.5cm (8in) from beg. With right side of work facing and using larger needles and **B**, pick up and k 39 sts along this marked section on left side. Rep 2nd rib row then keeping rib correct dec 1 st at lower edge on next 20 rows. Cont on rem 19 sts until work measures 13.5cm (5¼in) from beg, ending with a wrong-side row. Cut yarn and leave sts on a holder.

■ Work other side section along right edge of centre in same way, reversing shapings, and when this section measures same length ending with a wrong-side row cont as foll: work in rib across these 19 sts, cont in rib across 21 sts of centre section then cont in rib across 19 sts of left side section. 59 sts. Cont in rib across all sts for 9cm (3½in) then cast off in rib.

■ **Ears** With larger needles and **B** cast on 5 sts for outer section and work in rib but inc 1 st at both ends of every alt row 5 times. Cont on these 15 sts and work 6 rows straight then cast off in rib. For inner section cast on 5 sts using larger needles and **A**. Work in rib but inc 1 st at both ends of every alt row 4 times. Cont on these 13 sts and work 5 rows straight. Cast off in rib. Placing cast-off edges level sew inner and outer sections tog neatly. Sew back seams of hood and make a neat backstitch seam at centre front. Sew ears to top of hood. Complete features as

for pocket of sweater.

CAT

■ **Sweater** For back and front work as for sweater of Fox design using **A** for welts then change to larger needles and, working in st st, work in stripes of 4 rows **B**, 4 rows **A**; complete as for Fox design.

■ **Sleeves** Work as for Fox sweater but after completing cuff change to larger needles and work in st st in stripes as for back and front; inc 1 st at both ends of every foll 6th row 2(3-4) times then every foll 4th row 6(5-4) times.

■ Cont on these 47(50-53) sts until work measures 26(28-30)cm, 10¼(11-11¾)in, from beg, then cast off.

■ **Pocket** With larger needles and **B** cast on 4 (5-6) sts and work in st st; work 2 rows straight then inc 1 st at both ends of next 10 rows. Cont on 24 (25-26) sts until work measures 8(8-9)cm, 3⅛(3⅛-3½)in, from beg. Cast off.

■ With right side of work facing and using larger needles and **B**, pick up and k 19 (19-21) sts along right side edge of centre section. Rep 2nd rib row, then keeping rib correct shape both edges.

■ *1st row* Cast off 3, rib to last 8 sts, turn.

■ *2nd and alt rows* Rib to end.

■ *3rd row* Cast off 2, rib to last 7 sts, turn.

■ *5th row* Cast off 2, rib to last 6 sts, turn. Cont to cast off 2 sts at beg of every alt row and work 1 extra st before turning at end of same row 3 (3-4) times more. Work 1 row in rib on rem 6 sts then cast off in rib.

■ Work similar border along other side reversing shapings.

■ **Ears** With larger needles and **A** cast on 3 sts for outer section and work in rib but inc 1 st at both ends of every alt row 3 times then cont on 9 sts for 6 rows. Cast off in rib. For inner section cast on 3 sts using larger needles and **B**; work in rib but inc 1 st at both ends of every alt row twice then cont on 7 sts for 5 rows. Cast off in rib. Holding cast-off edges level sew

inner and outer sections tog neatly. Sew ears to top of pocket and sew pocket to centre front of sweater just above welt. Embroider nose in pink yarn. Cut whiskers and pass through base of pocket. Sew on eyes.

■ **Hood** For centre section cast on 5 sts using larger needles and **B**. Beg with a k row work in st st for 9 rows then inc 1 st at both ends of next 5 rows. 15 sts. Now work in stripes of 4 rows **A**, 4 rows **B**; cont to inc 1 st at both ends of next 5 rows then cont on these 25 sts until work measures 35cm (13¾in) from beg, ending with a p row. Cut yarn and leave these sts on a holder.

■ On each side edge of this section mark a point 6cm (2⅜in) from beg. With right side of work facing and using larger needles and **B**, pick up and k 13 sts along right side edge on marked section. Rep 2nd rib row then keeping rib correct shape both edges. Cast off 2 sts at beg of next row and next 5 alt rows – these shapings are at lower edge – *and at same time* inc 1 st at opposite edge on every alt row 5 times then cast on 15 sts at same edge on next alt row. 21 sts. Cont in rib without shaping for 18cm (7⅛in) ending with a wrong-side row. Cut yarn and leave sts on a holder. Work other side section in same way reversing shapings. With right side facing and using larger needles and **B**, rib sts of first side section, then cont in rib across sts of centre section then rib sts of second side section. Cont on these 67 sts and work in rib for 10cm (4in). Cast off in rib. Join side seams and make a neat backstitch seam at centre front.

■ **Ears** For outer section cast on 3 sts using larger needles and **A**; work in rib but inc 1 st at both ends of every alt row 4 times then work 6 rows straight. Cast off in rib. For inner section cast on 3 sts using larger needles and **B**; work in rib but inc 1 st at both ends of every alt row 3 times. Work 5 rows straight then cast off in rib. Assemble ears as for pocket, sew to top of hood. Complete features as for pocket.

STOCKISTS

If you have difficulty obtaining the specified yarns in your area, the stockists listed below may be able to help you, either by supplying the yarn directly to you or by giving you the name of your local supplier.

DMC
For mail order suppliers of DMC yarns, send a SAE to:
DMC Creative World Ltd, Pullman Road, Wigston, Leicester LE8 2DY. Tel: 0533 811040

JONELLE
John Lewis stocks a range of 4-ply, double knit and alpaca blend double knit yarns.
John Lewis, Oxford Street, London W1A 1EX.
Tel: 071 629 7711

PATONS
Patons and Baldwins Ltd, Knitting Queries Dept, Alloa, Scotland SK10 1EG. Tel: 0259 723431

PHILDAR UK LTD
For a list of stockists, send a SAE to:
Smallwares Ltd, 2 Peary Street, Rochdale Road, Manchester M60 4BW. Tel: 061 8343371

PINGOUIN
French Wools Ltd, Station House, 81-83 Fulham High Street, London SW6 3JW. Tel: 071 371 5773

ROWAN
For a list of stockists, send a SAE to:
Rowan Yarns, Green Lane Mill, Holmfirth, Huddersfield, W. Yorkshire HD7 1RW.

SIRDAR
Sirdar plc, Flanshaw Lane, Alverthorpe, Wakefield, Yorkshire WF2 9ND. Tel: 0924 371501

SOPHIE DESROCHES
Available by mail order from:
Naturally Beautiful Dent, 20 Brassey Road, Winchester, Hants SO22 6SB. Tel: 0962 861407

WENDY
Carter and Parker Ltd, Netherfield Road, Guiseley, Yorkshire LS20 9PD. Tel: 0943 72264

Acknowledgments (Photographer/Stylist)
1 G. de Chabaneix/I. Garçon
4-21 G. de Chabaneix/C. de Chabaneix
22-24 D Burgi/A. de Chabaneix-Luntz
26-27 G. de Chabaneix/C. de Chabaneix
30-32 M. Duffas/I. Garçon
34-37 G. de Chabaneix/C. de Chabaneix
38-45 G. de Chabaneix/I. Garçon
49-57 G. de Chabaneix/C. de Chabaneix
58-61 G. de Chabaneix/I. Garçon
62-67 G. de Chabaneix/C. de Chabaneix
68-71 G. de Chabaneix/I. Garçon
72-79 G. de Chabaneix/A. de Chabaneix